"Chris Taylor's book is packed with sound, practical advice on how to build a successful, low cost, business in direct sales. Around the world, network marketing is now accepted as the modern way of organising direct selling business. It offers substantial rewards to any new distributor based on just two activities - their personal retail sales and the retail sales achievements of those teams of direct sellers that they have recruited, motivated and trained to follow their own example - all of whom have exactly the same opportunity to build their own substantial businesses. I'm confident that Chris' book will help get this important message across to a much wider audience."

Richard Berry, Director
The Direct Selling Association

What people are saying about this book!

"Chris Taylor has found The Formula for Success and shares it in a clear and helpful way in this great book, a must read for anyone wanting to succeed in Network Marketing."

Brian Mayne,
Inspirational coach & author of 'Goal Mapping'

"In the decade that I have known him, I have watched Chris Taylor develop and put into practice his unique formula for success. In doing so, he has helped countless people to achieve things which they never believed themselves capable. This formula is relevant and duplicatable in all networks across the industry, as it contains the basic principles that are essential to building and growing a team. "

David Barber
Author of 'Just what is Network Marketing?'

"The ultimate book has now been written! 'The Formula For Success in Network Marketing' presents everything for both the would be network marketer, who is perhaps looking for a better understanding of the business and deciding if the industry is for themselves, but also for the many thousands of people already working within the industry, who for whatever reason are not enjoying the rewards that they feel they should be.

Contained within this book is the clear message that success within this industry is for anyone who chooses it, and also a clear plan of essential actions and activities that ensure it happens. If you are serious about becoming successful in MLM, you cannot afford not to read this book!"

Trevor Wagstaff
Managing Director
Brian Tracy International UK

What people are saying about this book!

"Believe me, we've read a lot of books, suggested for helping the networker to build a network. Your book tops them all; it is straightforward, easy to understand, and relatable in terms of a networker's life and business experience - it speaks to them!" - VK

"I honestly think this is going to be the best tool any networker could have. It was interesting for me because I was reading about a system that I KNOW WORKS - I think it will be even more interesting for those who've never come across it before, to do and to experience the benefit of having such a tool." - KK

"This great industry loses far too many people who were closer to success than they realised before they quit. The real life, practical help that this book gives, will make all the difference, and help people achieve far more than they ever thought possible." - CD

"This book is a fantastic step-by-step guide to building an incredible network, business & future. Follow it & you can't fail. The information isn't only brilliant in theory but it works! Having the pleasure of working with the author, I've put this formula into practice & have seen the results in my own network. Let this book guide you - it's all there. All you need to do is commit to it." - CL

"We have been involved with two network marketing companies over the last twelve years, each with very different levels of success.

In our first network, the company philosophy and group system were almost totally focused on motivation, excitement, positivity and seeing the 'big picture'.

Now, whilst all of these factors are crucial to building a successful networking business, the most fundamental thing got missed out - what to do and how to do it! We were never taught the practical nuts and bolts of putting the business together and working effectively with people.

However, when we joined our current organisation, things changed. From Day One, Chris taught us a practical and effective system of building a network that would easily duplicate itself and build strength in depth.

A confused distributor will not build a successful business, and we firmly believe that Chris' book, which encapsulates his successful system, will clarify everything. This book contains fundamental principles that can be applied by any networker, in any organisation, regardless of their level of experience.

We have known Chris for nearly 10 years now, and have become firm friends with him during this time. Without his help, support and guidance, our own success would not have been possible." SB

The Formula for Success in Network Marketing

by Chris Taylor

www.the-formula-for-success.com

Published in the UK by
Filament Publishing Ltd
14 Croydon Road, Waddon,
Croydon, Surrey CR0 4PA
Telephone +44 (0) 208 688 2598

info@filamentpublishing.com
www.filamentpublishing.com

ISBN 978-1-905493-19-7

Printed and bound in Great Britain by CPI Antony Rowe Chippenham & Eastbourne and in the USA

Free downloads of the worksheets featured in this book, plus ordering information, can be found on www.the-formula-for-success.com

For my wife and children,
my reason for building this fabulous business.

I would also like to dedicate this book
to everyone in network marketing,
for making this wonderful industry possible.

Foreword from The Author

This book is for everyone in network marketing needing a way to help them build their business faster and more time efficiently than they are currently able to. For years, I waited for a book like this to arrive on the market and, as it hasn't, I finally decided to write it myself.

However, after much thought I've decided to write under a pen name. I'm very active at a high level in my network, and I'm enjoying significant success. My network marketing organisation turnover is millions of pounds a year. My income is in the top 5% in the UK and I am semi-retired 25 years early.

My family and I enjoy the wonderful lifestyle that a royalty income can give us. We have the money and the time to enjoy spending it. Among the amazing things we have been able to do was to realise a long standing dream and enjoy a six month holiday.

I've been invited to speak on the networking industry on several television programmes. I have also spoken on radio, had multiple press releases and I regularly train at national and international events organised by my network marketing company.

I know you want to know which network, but to be honest, it's not relevant. I want you to focus on and learn from the information you are about to read. The message is far more important than the messenger and I believe knowing the name of my network would be a distraction.

This book is about the fundamental principles of building a successful network marketing business, which I've learned through trial and error building both my current and previous networks.

Over the years I've helped thousands of people to achieve their goals with these principles. They are applicable to all networks and I know you can achieve your goals if you put the information you are about to read into action.

'The Formula For Success In Network Marketing' is a step by step guide to building a successful network marketing business. There is a wealth of information to help every networker, from the point of just starting out with no networking experience, to the more advanced strategies needed by seasoned networkers with a large team keen to progress at a quicker speed.

I have written this book so it can be read in its entirety and put into action, step by step. Or, once you are following these principles you can dip into it and refresh yourself on a particular point as you need it. You may need to adapt the diagram sheets in this book to fit your network. However, do not leave a step out. The activities necessary to build a network marketing business are like the spokes of a wheel. If you remove even one spoke, the wheel becomes weaker and may eventually collapse.

Enjoy reading this book, enjoy this wonderful industry, enjoy building your business and enjoy the amazing lifestyle that results from putting this knowledge into action.

Chris Taylor

Table of Contents

Diagram Index

Chapter 1

Network Marketing is a Great Industry

Network marketing is the best industry in the world. I view it as the people's franchise. There is no other industry that touches it. Your business start-up costs are minimal, you work it part-time around a job or other commitments and there is no financial risk to yourself or your family.

The concept of network marketing is brilliant. The parent company takes care of the corporate side of the business for its distributors, ie, product purchases and development, overheads, premises, deliveries, etc, so that we, the distributors, can concentrate on income generating activities. The parent company is a warehouse and they excel at that side of the business. Can you imagine what it would be like if you had to hold stock and work out what sells and what doesn't sell, as you would if you owned a conventional business? As a distributor you have no stock, no staff and no premises.

Distributors sell the parent company's products and find new distributors to sell the products. The company then pays its distributors the money a conventional business would use for activities such as advertising on TV and in newspapers, branding their products and the salaries of sales reps because these are the activities which are undertaken by its distributors.

Essentially a network marketing company pays a significant percentage of the money it receives from the sale of its products to the distributors who sell them.

Network marketing is a financial vehicle and without question the number one way to build a business.

Many distributors earn £300+ a month in their spare time. This is like having a pay rise of £3,600 per annum. How many people do you know who have had a pay rise of £300 a month?

Apart from creating an excellent part-time income, networks are designed for ordinary people to achieve extraordinary incomes with no prior training. Most people start their network marketing business looking for an extra income of a few extra pounds a month on top of their ordinary income and then realise the potential of building a business. Many networkers, in my organisation and all over the world, have achieved their dream, sacked their boss and are now earning their income entirely from network marketing. You have the opportunity to earn a seriously huge income. The sky is the limit. I hope this is giving you food for thought. What income would you like to be earning in the next 5 years?

As an employee, have you ever overtaken the wage of your boss? The payment system in network marketing is very fair. New distributors have the potential to earn far more money than the person who sponsored them. The person who builds the bigger business earns more money.

There is no other industry where you can start a business for only a few hundred pounds, meaning you don't need to re-mortgage your house. It is totally flexible so you can run it part-time alongside a job, family or other commitments and it enables you to earn a fantastic income. You have no staff, you can take time off when you choose and once you have built it securely you can leave town and still earn a royalty income.

People join a network marketing business for many different reasons. In my organisation I have people who work full-time, for example, company directors, teachers, shop clerks and people who have full-time commitments like single parent mothers. Many of these people are looking for a change of lifestyle, a taste of success, a new challenge or friendship as well as an extra income.

You don't even need a car. I have a very successful distributorship in my organisation who didn't have a car when they joined. They built a massive team and still choose not to own a car!

Network marketing is recession proof. In fact, a downturn in the national economy is a great time to be in a network because more people are looking for an extra income to pay the bills.

Your future with network marketing is amazing. You need to be focused, you need to have a great work ethic and you need to have dedication to your goals. Move network marketing from your head, into your heart. Have passion for your business, passion for the networking industry, passion for your goals and passion for what you really want to achieve with your business. Passion will give you enthusiasm and confidence and you will achieve your goals if you truly desire them.

So why do some people build a really big network marketing business? And why is it some people don't? The obvious answer is that some people simply don't want to build a big business! They may be happy with their income and their lifestyle and there is nothing wrong with that. There are also many people who acknowledge they are not prepared to work really hard today to have a different future. They simply don't want to do the work. The remaining people are those who want a better, more financially secure future and are actively trying to achieve it.

You will come across people who tell you network marketing doesn't work. You need to know they simply don't understand it. They are not ready to join your business yet. Just keep moving on and find other people to work with.

Throughout my network marketing career I have also spoken to many people who, in their ignorance, have told me that network marketing doesn't work. I have one very memorable story from my early days in the business.

I prospected one of my family members telling him that I'd earned £310 in my first month and I asked him if he wanted to earn an income with network marketing, too. He told me, "*These things don't work* !" He obviously didn't realise there were thousands of people already earning an income through network marketing. So I decided to prove him wrong. If other people were making money, I could as well.

This family member said he would join when I was earning £2,000 a month, but when I showed him a cheque for £2,000 he decided it would only be temporary. Nine months later I agreed with him because my monthly cheque had risen to £4,000. Later on, once my income had exceeded £10,000 per month he said I'd been lucky! With mock horror I said to him, "*If you had told me this a few years ago I wouldn't have worked so hard* ! "

Building a network is a choice. Look at it this way. If you work for someone else you have to do the work anyway, until you retire. Choose to work for yourself. Think about what you have in your hands with network marketing.

Chapter 2

Persistence or Luck?

"You don't pay the price for success,
you pay the price for failure.
You enjoy the benefits of success." **Zig Ziglar**

I was recently having lunch with two friends. One of them is a successful millionaire with a thriving truck and lorry rental business. During the conversation I asked him what attributes he considered were necessary if someone wants to become successful. This is part of his reply;

"You have to be very persistent. Obviously you will get a lot of rejection but you've just got to keep going and keep going!"

When he started his conventional business he re-mortgaged his house and bought a few trucks. This was high risk for him. He started his business full-time and with no outside income, unlike a network marketing business. If he had failed he could have lost his house, and this is typical of anyone starting up their own conventional business.

He now has many trucks which he rents out to big companies, but when he first started he can't remember the number of companies he contacted where people said "*No, no, no!*" He became successful because he kept going until he achieved his goal. Our other friend immediately turned to him and said, "*You've been lucky!*" Before I could say anything he replied, "*No, it's not luck. It's hard work.*"

You need the same attributes to be successful in a conventional business as you do in a network marketing business. Successful people in any industry will tell you that you have to make your own luck!

LUCK stands for Labour Under Correct Knowledge!

You do not need luck in this business to become successful. If someone believes they need to be lucky it's usually the reason they are not growing as quickly as they would like to. Building a business does not require luck. It needs tunnel vision, focused activity and lots and lots of practice.

A while ago one of my down-line was having major challenges with sponsoring. He was talking to a lot of prospects but he wasn't able to sponsor anyone and he got really frustrated. He could have quit but he kept going, continually improving his technique and his attitude. Suddenly he sponsored 15 people in one month. He had distributors to work with and his business exploded. Everybody who builds a big network marketing business goes through this. You have to be persistent.

If you've been in your business for a while and you haven't got as far as you would like, but you are still involved and still trying, it shows you have leadership qualities and strength of character. You have not given up on your future. It's a glimpse of the person you can become.

Becoming a success in network marketing is just a decision away. Make the decision to be persistent and consistent, while building your business, until you have reached your goal. It amazes me how much can be done in just a few hours each day with the correct discipline.

Make the decision to actually work for the income you truly desire and make the decision, in your heart, to do whatever it takes to move your business forward.

Chapter 3

Royalty Income

Many people begin a network marketing business to earn a few extra £'s a week. However, once they attend a training or read a book they realise just how much this industry could change their lives and they adjust their goals. Their reason for building a business changes to earning a royalty income and 'owning their life'.

Before joining network marketing I had a thriving conventional business which took up a lot of my time and gave me all the headaches of a conventional business. I had many conversations with people of retirement age, people who were older and wiser than me, and a lot of them were in financial difficulties at 65. They couldn't afford to live a good lifestyle and I realised I didn't want to end up like this. I didn't want to be broke at the age of 65. I wanted to own my life.

With my conventional business I also came into contact with a lot of wealthy people, and my perception of success changed. If someone has a lot of money but they keep going to work there is, in my opinion, something not quite right! I was discovering many people are broke at a higher level. They have the status symbols, ie, cars, houses and holidays, but they are in debt up to their eyeballs to pay for it.

My idea of success changed from people who have lots of money, to people who have plenty of money and the time to enjoy it. I needed a royalty income!

To me a royalty income means I don't have to get out of bed in the morning if I don't want to (although the children have different ideas!)

The royalty income gives me choices which I wouldn't have, if I had a job or a conventional business with a good income.

I made the decision, very early on, to do whatever it takes to build my network. No excuses! The lifestyle and income I now enjoy is a reward for all the hard work I put into building my business.

I worked really hard for 3 years. I had total tunnel vision and I gave it all I had. It wasn't a question of sign on the dotted line and do nothing. I really stretched myself and expanded my comfort zone. I was prepared to do more than the average person because I wanted to be ahead of the majority of people in the world. I wanted to excel at doing something which anyone could do, but not everyone was prepared to do, and I was willing to work hard to get it.

I put my business first, for 3 years, until my first child was born. Then I decided to take some time off. For the first time since I started my network marketing business, it was not my main priority. When I went back to it I put in less hours because I wanted to spend time with my son. This was one of my goals because as a child I saw very little of my father.

During the following 2 years I watched my income double as the momentum continued and the solid foundation which I had built by working so hard during the previous 3 years continued to expand my business.

Today I still work my network marketing business part-time, some evenings. I no longer have a conventional business and I choose to be a full-time family man. I earn a full royalty income, I own my life and when I work with my team it's because I choose to.

I still have business goals which I aspire to and I have a commitment to help the people in my organisation to achieve their goals. This is what drives me now.

I'm fully committed to helping other people to succeed. I earn a lot of money and I'm semi-retired 25 years early. However, I still love network marketing and I'm dedicated to helping other people to achieve success.

I have also made many friends along my journey in networking. Many of the people in my organisation, with whom I have worked closely, I no longer class as friends. They are more like an extended family!

I live my dream lifestyle. My family and I have the holidays, the houses, the cars, private education for the children and no rationing of treats. Everything is paid for up-front and nothing is purchased on credit. I'm telling you this to show you what is available to you if you build a business in this industry.

I'm not a motivator, I'm a trainer. I could motivate you until you are over-motivated and jumping up and down, but then in 2 hours you will stop jumping......., or I could teach you how to build a business. I believe that if someone is trained correctly they can actually achieve their dream lifestyle, too!

Once your network marketing business is built properly it continues to grow whether you are there or not. A royalty income allows you to choose what you want to do with your time and you truly own your life.

I have a lifestyle many people dream of achieving. They play the lottery every week and dream about what they would do with the money if they won. Amazingly, there are many people who want to win the lottery, but don't buy a ticket.

Network marketing takes the luck out of winning. If you focus you will achieve a big income and you can give your family and friends the same 100% chance to win.

Network marketing is a wonderful opportunity. Grab it with both hands and run with it all the way to the finishing line. You have already found the way to achieve your dream lifestyle. All you have to do now is work hard to achieve it.

Chapter 4

Do What It Takes

The basic concept of network marketing is to help other people to achieve what they want to achieve so you get what you want. If you want to make more money you have to, quite simply, do more activity and help more people to make money. How much you earn depends on your total group volume and the structure of your team. Building a network marketing business is a process of doing tasks repetitively, over and over again, until your business has reached the turnover you desire.

Many distributors think they need to personally sponsor and work with thousands of people to build a massive business. This isn't the case. The organisation you build will eventually have thousands of people, but you do not sponsor all these people yourself and you only work with one or two people at a time. Building your business is all about teaching and duplication. You teach your team to duplicate you and you leverage your time.

I would like to show you how simple the idea of network marketing is. Many people sponsor one person a week, but I will demonstrate to you how effective network marketing can be, even if you only sponsor one person a month.

If you sponsor one person a month, in one year, you would personally sponsor just 12 people. However, if you then teach

each of these people to sponsor one person a month, and to teach it, in 12 months you will have over 4,000 distributors in your group.

Diagram 1

Month			Team Total
1	you	+1 person sponsored by you	2 people
2	you +1	+2 new distributors	4 people
3	you +3	+4 new distributors	8 people
4	8	+8 new distributors	16
5	16	+16 new distributors	32
6	32	+32 new distributors	64
7	64	+64 new distributors	128
8	128	+128 new distributors	256
9	256	+256 new distributors	512
10	512	+512 new distributors	1024
11	1024	+1024 new distributors	2048
12	2048	+2048 new distributors	4096

Sponsoring one person a month isn't difficult. It depends on your activity level and your attitude.

What happens if you increase your sponsoring to two people a month?

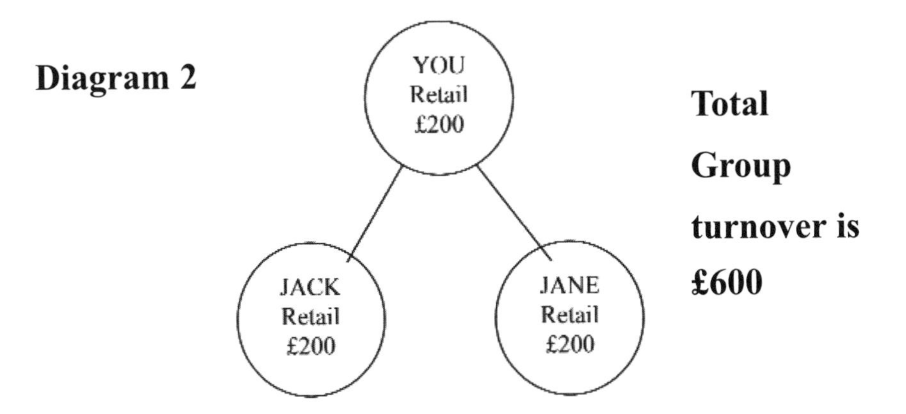

As an example, if you personally retail £200 of products every month and teach everyone you sponsor to duplicate you, at the end of your first month your group turnover will be £600. Your turnover has tripled, your income has increased and you have leveraged your time.

Following this principle, at the end of your first year your organisation's turnover would be phenomenal. Once you become focused and teach two people how to duplicate you, you have the knowledge to build a massive business and you can teach the principle.

However, before you get too excited, too quickly, I need to let you know that in the real world the first two people you sponsor may not duplicate you straightaway. Teaching them takes time and you will probably have to sponsor more people to find two people who want to sponsor and build a team immediately. Also, some people you introduce may just want to sell products and choose not to build a team at all.

Occasionally I've had people come to me and say they can't sponsor. The first question I ask them is how many contacts they talk to daily and weekly. You need to break down the activity you do to that degree. By speaking to just 5 people a day the count per week and per month mounts up.

Once you have a team beginning to build, you need to become a good leader. Leading from the front starts with promoting your products and product sales. You must sell products and build your own customer lists. The volume of products you personally sell is your choice. However, you need to remember that once you start to build a team, your team will duplicate your personal sales turnover and all the other business building activity you do. If you choose to retail little or no personal sales volume, you need to understand your group will eventually start to duplicate you and you will have a big team doing very little. Not everyone will do what you do, but the serious people will duplicate the serious leaders in their line of sponsorship.

I had one group in my organisation where the leader thought it was not necessary to sell products to grow a big business, and almost everyone in the team copied by doing little or no personal sales. There were over 100 people in this team and it barely qualified at the first main level in the marketing plan. In a different leg, with approximately the same number of people, the group leader did good personal sales and as a result, there was a large turnover.

If you want to build your business very quickly it's vital you create massive activity. You decide how much you want to do, but to achieve a high royalty income you need to create massive and sustained activity. This industry is all about activity, retailing, sponsoring and teaching on a regular and consistent basis. Focus fully on what needs to be done.

When you sponsor you are looking for one or two people who want to build this business as quickly as you do. Sponsoring is only a numbers game until you find someone to work with. Once you find someone, how you work with them will determine their success and, in turn, your success.

You need to know how to teach, coach and train your people effectively and, as you progress up the marketing plan in your business, how to work in depth with your distributors. I will cover 'working with your team' in a later chapter.

Your team members look at you and what you achieve. It's important you continue to move up the marketing plan as it gives your down-line belief you can help them to succeed. Continuously strive to move forward.

You must be honest with people. When you are the leader of a big team and you are coaching and developing new leaders tell them they will get people who drop out of their team and others who won't do what they said they would. Let them know they are the leader of their team. You have to help your leaders to move on and not to focus on small challenges.

You also have to be honest with yourself. If you haven't achieved your goal up to this point, your first step is to ask yourself whether you've really been doing what it takes to build your business. If you haven't up to now, you need to promise yourself to treat your business seriously from this day forward.

Make today a new beginning. Whether you have been in your business one week or five years, start afresh from today. What you achieve in your business will depend on your goals and what you want out of your business. It's important you start as you mean to go on. Retail your products, put action and energy into lead generation, sponsor new people and your business will begin to gather momentum.

Try to excel in every area of your business and be honest with yourself. If something isn't working, or needs improving, learn how to do it better. It's only by doing everything well (although not necessarily perfectly!) that your business will grow.

I'm not a special person and I don't excel at everything. I don't always get everything right first time but I learn by my mistakes. I don't have any school qualifications, but I did make the decision to work very, very hard in this fabulous industry.

There are millions of people who want to earn more money or change their lifestyle. If your group isn't as big as you would like it to be, or the people you have in your team are not moving as fast as you want them to move, find more people. I've had people in my organisation who were not ready to build a business for more than two years after registering as distributors. You need to keep moving on, because once you do people in your team will want to move on as well.

I'm going to share a story with you about a major event in my networking career. Seven months after I became involved in my network I had a small team and reached the first rung in my ladder of success. But at that point I got stuck at the same turnover for about a year and I became very frustrated. I blamed the down-line, and grumbled because they were not putting enough effort into their businesses!

Then, one morning, I woke up and realised it was not their fault. It was my fault. They had reached their goals. They hadn't actually said it to me but it is what happened.

So I moved on. I was there for them when they needed me but I stopped waiting for them. One year later my group turnover had reached six figures every month and I was winning awards from the company. I'd changed my focus and taken responsibility for my business.

It takes time to build a business and it won't be an overnight success. Network marketing isn't a get rich quick scheme. You need to understand that a royalty income doesn't appear overnight. It takes two to five years of consistent, focused work to be in a secure financial situation and to totally own your life.

You need to measure how long you've been in your business by how much time you've been working it properly. This begins on the day you actually decide to get serious and focus on your business. If you've already been involved for a year, but you haven't been focused, you can't count it. A solid business takes two to five years of hard work and effort.

Chapter 5

Challenges and Education

I believe a winner is someone who overcomes challenges and keeps moving forward. They are someone you can admire and,once they earn a big income, think back and say, "*I remember when they weren't earning big money and the challenges which they overcame!*"

As you are building your business you will come across challenges. Nobody builds a substantial business, either network marketing or conventional, without challenges. However, challenges are only a problem if you perceive them to be. It's not the challenge which makes a difference to the speed you build your business, but how you react to it.

When you have a challenge you need to work through it. Nothing is impossible, it just takes a special effort. You need to treat it as a learning curve. Overcome challenges and learn from them.

Building a network is an emotional rollercoaster for everyone. We all go through it. Building my business has not been a walk in the park and I've had many occasions when I've wanted to pull my hair out in frustration. Success is not determined by how many times your mental attitude goes up and down, but by how long you spend in a negative frame of mind when you are in a dip.

When things are going well it's easy to have a good attitude. However it's not so easy when things are not going well. This is when we need to go to work on our attitude. Always try to have a positive outlook.

Answer these questions;

When you look at a cup is it half full or half empty?

What sort of attitude do you wake up with in the morning?

What attitude do you have when you make business phone calls?

When you do your follow-ups don't have the 'stinking thinking attitude', ie, "*I'll have to talk to a load of clowns this evening*!" If you think this way you will find yourself talking to a load of clowns. Have a positive attitude. Believe you will talk to people who want to join your business.

Having the correct attitude is crucial. It's the difference between 'Maybe I will succeed' and 'I will succeed, I'm determined to do it'. You have to believe in yourself. Remember the old adage;

If you believe you can,
you can.
If you believe you can't,
you are probably right.

This is so true. You must believe you can build your business. When you get up in the morning and look in the mirror what do you see? You should be looking at a winner. Your self-talk should be,

"I am a winner. I believe I can. I have made the decision to build a big business and achieve my goals. I am doing what it takes for myself and for my family."

Is this what you hear? You have to make the decision to move forward.

When you feel your positive attitude slipping a little, ask yourself,

"What am I doing correctly?"

Focus on this and work on the bits which need adjusting so that you become more effective.

You can help yourself to reduce the effects of your emotional rollercoaster by educating yourself. Read books and listen to CD's.

You should read for at least 15 minutes a day. If you think you don't have that much time, here are some suggestions. Get up a little earlier. Read on the toilet in the morning...., positive in, negative out! Read on the train, waiting for the bus, or in your lunch hour. Network marketing is about earning a small income while you learn how to build a big one. You earn while you learn.

I didn't like school and the last thing I wanted to do when I got into network marketing was to read, but I did. I had to learn to be a reader because I didn't enjoy it. I forced myself to read a page a day because I knew I wouldn't be where I am today if I didn't get myself educated. I knew regular reading and self-development was very important. Even with the royalty income I have now I still read and I'm still learning and developing.

Self-development is crucial if you want your business to grow. Your business will only grow when you develop as a person. People who achieve, self-develop every day.

Listen to CD's while you are driving. Turn your car into an open university. Self-development is simple to achieve.

Once you start getting emotional and frustrated with your business, self-development through CD's and books is very important.

Put the information you learn through self-development into action. Information is like driving a car. You may have the fastest car in the world but it won't drive itself. You have to get into the car and drive it to make it move. Self-development is similar. You may know what to do to grow your business, but if you don't put the information you learn into action, it will slow your growth.

Use your personal development to become the person who earns the income you want to earn. What do I mean by that? If you were earning your goal income right now, maybe £5,000 or £10,000 every month, what sort of attitude would you have? What sort of posture would you have? Become the person who is earning this income, today.

Here is an example. If you want to reach step 5 in your marketing plan you need to be putting the amount of effort into your business, right now, that you think someone who is at step 5 in your marketing plan would be putting into their business in order to continue to build and move on to the next level. Your focus and work rate need to be ahead of your actual status in the marketing plan. Ask yourself what level in your marketing plan you are currently working at right now?

You can't wait until you reach a level in your business before you start putting in the effort which is required in order to reach it. You will never get there. Focus on the level you want to achieve in your business and then put in the effort to achieve it.

Once you get focused and do this you will become a magnet for success. You will attract people who want to become as successful as you are. Things will start to happen. People will actually ring you to join your business.

Chapter 6

Prioritising

If you want to be successful you have to do what successful people did to become successful!

When you are talking to someone who is doing massive activity it may appear they are working too hard, especially if you are not doing enough in your own business at the moment. However you need to understand that their work rate is dictated by their goals. They have massive goals and they are in a hurry to achieve them.

There is a saying,

Ask someone busy to do something and it will be done.

Most people in network marketing, who built a big group, did it on a part-time basis. They fitted everything they needed to do into the few hours they had available to them each day to build their business. Successful people prioritise so that they can become successful.

Everybody has 24 hours in each day, and if you want to build your business quickly you need to learn to prioritise your life. Building a network takes time management skills. How you choose to use your 24 hours each day will determine how successful your business will be and what income you will earn. Luxuries and a great lifestyle take commitment.

You may need to put some of the things you enjoy doing on the back-burner for a while. Spend less time doing non-business building activities. Television can be a major time waster. If you like watching TV, record your programme and watch it later. This way you won't be tempted to sit in front of the television for hours, or to watch it instead of doing phone calls during 'primetime'.

Working this hard is only temporary. Within a few years, once you have built your own network marketing business, you can choose what you want to do with the rest of your life.

Do you choose temporary inconvenience for long-term convenience? It's a serious decision!

If someone wants to do something badly enough they will find the time. Many people who have children choose to work nights so they can spend time with their family. They make their family a priority. Decide to make your network marketing business a priority.

One lady in my organisation has two jobs outside of her networking business, she has children and she is still selling products and sponsoring people. She finds the time because it is important to her.

People generally don't have a time problem, they have a priority problem.

Chapter 7

Trainings

Training isn't unique to network marketing. If you want to earn a phenomenal income in any industry, whether you have your own conventional business, or you are a doctor, a lawyer or a barrister, you need to have training. Network marketing is no different. Trainings are there to teach you how to build your business.

Attend all training events. This is very important. You should treat a training event as if you had spent £1,000 on the ticket. I've known team members, in the past, who chose not to attend a training because they had the weekend off and they didn't get many weekends off with their job. My attitude is, and has always been, take a day off in the week from your job and attend the training. Your J.O.B. (Just Over Broke) will not give you financial independence or the time to enjoy your money. Network marketing can, and you learn how to build your network marketing business at trainings.

When you are excited and things are going well, you need to attend a training to understand and learn how to build your business.

When you are feeling low and negative you need to attend a training to understand and learn how to build your business!

The time when you least feel like going to a training is the time that attending a training will do you the most good. When you are feeling low and your attitude is taking a dip, learn from other people who understand the challenges you are experiencing. They may be able to give you tips on how to overcome them. Talking to other people will make you feel better and increase your confidence. Everyone has felt like this at one time or another.

Some people who attend trainings think their business will build naturally, simply because they went to it. It doesn't work that way. When you attend a training you must take notes, review your notes and put them into action. Being teachable is absolutely imperative. Attending won't do you or your business any good at all unless you learn from the information you receive.

You should have a note journal which you take to every training and refer to it when you need information. Note taking does not mean copying a speech down word for word. You write bullet points on the information you perceive is being delivered.

If there are two of you in partnership in your business, you should both be taking copious notes. When we go to a training my wife and I each take our own notes. Information in a training will mean different things to different people, and each person needs different information to progress with their business.

During training breaks use the time to talk to people, especially new people, and hear as many stories as you can. Then, when you speak to other people, share your story and the recent positive stories you have heard with them.

Once you have a team you need to become the best promoter of trainings in your business. The more team members you have attending the faster your business will grow.

If someone in your team won't come to trainings they are not going to build a business. Without training, it doesn't matter how much personal sales volume they do a month, being active in their business will only be short-term and temporary. Most people join network marketing because they want to earn a royalty income, not to have a job as a sales person for the network marketing company they work with.

It's important you do everything you can to get your team to attend trainings. Many people don't attend trainings when they first join network marketing. Keep an eye on them. Send them newsletters, training CD's and communicate regularly. Explain that they will receive information at training events to help them to run their business more effectively, and stress the importance of attending at least one training even if they just want to sell products. Keep encouraging them, but work with other people. Constant communication will eventually give them belief. Once they have belief in themselves and in the company they will travel and do whatever it takes to build their business.

I had one gentleman in my organisation called Paul. Paul was a phenomenal retailer but he wouldn't come to trainings, he wasn't on voicemail so communication was difficult and he wasn't plugging into the system. After 2 years of phenomenal retail he got a job because he didn't see the bigger picture.

Having many members of your team altogether at the same event, for example, at trainings, any group lead-generating activities such as flyering, or team socials like a meal, barbeque or bowling is very important because it gels your team together. It creates a bond between people. Group events generate excitement and laughter, which in turn creates motivation and momentum in your business. People get more done when they are enjoying building their business.

Chapter 8

Goals

Many people spend more time planning their holiday, than they spend planning their future!

Your first step in running a successful business is setting your goals. Running a business without goals is like playing a football match without goal posts! Goals give you direction. They are your reason for building your business. You need to know what you want to achieve so you can plan what you need to do to achieve it!

Clearly defined goals will keep you going on the days when you think things are going badly and you are feeling low. You need to decide what you want to achieve and break it down into smaller manageable chunks. Then, you need to write a plan of action to achieve your goal.

You can have business goals, for example, how much money you want to earn, where you want to be in your marketing plan, and can you see yourself speaking in public, or you can have personal goals like a bigger house, a better car, subscriptions to charity, private education for the children or holidays for the family.

You also need to understand that goals are not fixed. As you progress through your business you need to keep re-setting your goals. When you get close to achieving one goal, aim for the next one so you have something to focus on once you achieve the goal you are currently going for. This is crucial. If you don't have a new goal to go for you will have nothing to focus on and your business will lose momentum.

When you first try to set your goals it can be difficult because it's not something people are taught at school.

Your first step is to decide what you want to achieve in your business and how you see your lifestyle in 5 or 10 years time. This is your ultimate goal. You will also want smaller things like a holiday, a car, pay off debts or dinner for two in a restaurant, etc.

The goals you choose should be things you feel strongly about. You need to have emotions attached to wanting something. One reason for having goals is to help you to overcome challenges and to drive you to do the activity which will enable your business to grow. Nothing kicks into place unless your reason for building a big business is rock solid.

Once you know what you want to achieve the next step is to decide when you want to achieve it by. Goals are only a wish list until you put a date on them.

Don't be afraid to have big goals or a desire to achieve them quickly. My goals have always been clear, precise and very big. I made myself stretch, and in doing so there were goals I achieved and goals which I missed in the time frame I had set for myself. However, even though I missed some, I was a lot closer to achieving my ultimate goal than when I started!

When choosing your goals, don't go for goals you think you *should* want, only those you definitely *do* want. If there are two of you in a partnership you need to make sure they are your own goals and not your partner's. You need to have separate goals, although some goals may be shared.

For example, a small goal for the wife to get her hair done is unlikely to drive the husband to build their business.

You need to split your goals into short, medium and long-term goals. A short-term goal is something you want to achieve in 1-6 months. A medium-term goal would have a date on it of 6 months to 2 years and long-term goals would be 2 to 5+ years.

The next step is to write your goals down, along with the date you want to achieve them by. Write your goals in the present tense as though you have already achieved them. This increases your ability to succeed because you are using positive thinking. You may have just a few goals, or as many as 10 or 15. Write them all down.

First write a statement of intent or your ultimate goal, if you like. This a picture of how you want your life to be in 5 to 10 years. This is an example;

I earn a royalty income of £30,000 per month.
I live in my dream house, a 4 bedroom country cottage.
I drive a red Porsche Boxter with cream leather interior.
My children attend Princes College, a private school.
I have a villa on the French Riviera and 6 holidays a year.

30 June 2014.

Visualise your life on this date. Know the details. See the colours, smell the scenery and hear the sounds. The stronger you visualise a goal, the more powerful it will be when you are using it to keep you going with your activity.

For a goal to work, you have to make it as clear and alive as possible. For instance, if you want a new car choose the make, the model, the colour, the interior and any optional extras. Then, go to a dealer and take a test drive! Sit in it! What are your emotions? Know how owning your new car would make you feel. Keep a picture and focus on what you need to do to achieve your goal.

After writing down your ultimate goal you need to add your short and medium-term goals. These are smaller goals which will keep you focused and let you know you are on your way to achieving your long-term goals. Examples of these may be;

I earn £300 per month from my business, end Jan 2010

I own a Vauxhall Corsa, end Nov 2011

Add business goals

Add Charity goals

Goals are powerful if you use them correctly. They will drive you to put energy into your activity. By focusing on your goals you use them to assist you in building your business. I'm going to share with you some of the strategies you should use to regularly remind yourself of your goals.

Carry your goals with you everywhere you go.

Write your goals on a business card sized piece of paper. Use it to focus yourself on doing the activity you have planned. Read your goal card regularly. You should definitely read it first thing every morning and last thing before you go to bed. Also, read it several other times during the day, particularly before business building activities, or if you are feeling low and wondering why you are doing a certain activity. It will keep you focused and remind you of your reasons for building your business.

Make a goal board.

Pin pictures and photos on it representing your goals, and attach dates. Place the board in a prominent place in your house so that you see it regularly. You can also go one step further and place pictures of each goal you are working towards all over your house, in your car or on your desk at work, so you can always see a visual aid of the next goal you will achieve. Use your goals to drive you into staying focused and doing the activity you need to do.

Once you know what your short, medium and long-term goals are you need to break them down again. Add smaller stepping stone goals, 1 or 2 a month. These are rewards for yourself and your family for achieving a small step along the way. This will give you a taste of success and the encouragement to keep going when it's difficult to see your long-term goal. By rewarding yourself you are able to keep your long-term goal in sight.

Examples of stepping stone goals are meals out with the family, a day trip, an evening in with a nice bottle of wine, or simply a few hours to switch off, relax and do as you please. I have people in my organisation who decided one of their stepping stone goals would be a new washing machine, a trip to the cinema and even a new pair of socks.

Finally, break it down even further. Write a monthly, weekly and daily plan of activity which will enable you to achieve your goals. Then you need to track the activity you actually do so you can check whether you are on target to achieve your goals, every step of the way.

Chapter 9

Planning Your Activity

"If you fail to plan, you plan to fail"

Planning is a very important activity when building a successful business, either conventional or in network marketing.

Plan your activity backwards. For example, if your goal is to earn £2,000 per month in 24 months time, you need to know how much you will be earning per month in 21 months time and 18 months time, etc. How much activity do you need to do to achieve your monthly targets?

Plan your weekly activity so you will achieve your weekly, monthly and quarterly business goals. Break it down.
You need to know three things;

i) **How many people you need to sponsor each week / month,**

ii) **How many people you need to talk to or show your business to, in order to sponsor these people, and**

iii) **How much lead generating activity you need to do each week to generate these contact leads.**

Your business building activities should be focused and there are several strategies you can use to make yourself more efficient. The first and most important is to use a daily planner. At a glance, it allows you to easily see what you should be doing to achieve your goals on time. Every time you complete an hour of business activity, as detailed on your planner, you will know you are one step closer to achieving your goal.

'Diagram 3' is an example of a blank seven day planner which you can personalise. It shows you what you should be doing every hour of each day, from the time you get up in the morning to the time you go to bed.

Start by blocking out areas of each day when you have things to do which are not business related. For example, if you work 9 to 5 and have a half-hour commute, you are tied up with work 08:30 - 17:30. Don't forget, a lot of activity can be achieved during a lunch hour.

Then you need to include personal time, family time and time for housework, etc. What is left is time you have available for building your business.

Fill in all the activities you have to do on a weekly basis. You should set time for lead generating activity, telephone calls, showing people your business, product sales, personal development and attending training meetings. Don't forget to add a half-hour slot on Saturday or Sunday evening to plan the following week.

Make the time slots for each activity realistic. The first plan you write will probably not be a success and you may need to adjust it for a few weeks before it becomes a realistic workable plan.

Some people choose to write their first plan back to front. Spend your first week writing down every activity you do, every minute of each day. Include personal and business activities.

At the end of the first week, check how long each activity took you and write a successful workable planner for the following week, with the correct timings for each activity. If you do this, in the first week you must make sure you do all the activity you planned to do, so you remain on target to achieve your goals.

Having goals is very important, but you won't achieve them unless you put in the necessary action. The planner is only an effective time management tool if you stick to it. Make sure you do what your planner says you need to do. For example, if your planner says you need to make 15 phone calls to people on your contact list on Tuesday between 7 and 8 o'clock, you must make those phone calls. If you don't, you will fall behind in your actual activity.

Leaders put their plan into action immediately.
No excuses.
Nothing can get in the way of what they need to do.

Other ways of focusing daily / weekly activity include visual aids and time management skills.

Example of a visual aid
On the Sunday evening when you write your planner, also make up the number of information packs you plan to post out the following week. As you post them throughout the week, you will see the pile reducing in size. You have a visual indication of how many leads you are doing. You can also do this with many other forms of activity.

Example of time management
Every night before you go to bed, write a list of the things you need to do the following day, in their order of importance. It will help you to remain focused on the important activities of the following day and ensure that the things you have to do urgently will be achieved.

Diagram 3

Weekly Planner

Date	Monday	Tuesday	Wednesday	Thursday	Friday	Saturday	Sunday
07:00 - 08:00							
08:00 - 09:00							
09:00 - 10:00							
10:00 - 11:00							
11:00 - 12:00							
12:00 - 13:00							
13:00 - 14:00							
14:00 - 15:00							
15:00 - 16:00							
16:00 - 17:00							
17:00 - 18:00							
18:00 - 19:00							
19:00 - 20:00							
20:00 - 21:00							
21:00 - 22:00							
22:00 - 23:00							

Chapter 10

Tracking Your Activity

A rocket going to the moon is off course most of the time. It constantly tracks its position, and adjusts and corrects its course, so it can achieve its goal and reach the moon.

You need to do the same with your business. Once you have planned your week and done your activity you need to track what you have achieved.

Did you do what you planned to do this week?

Are you still on target to reach your goals?

When you compare the activity you planned, with the activity you actually did, you know whether you are still on target. If your actual activity is equal to, or more than, you planned to do you will gain a 'feel good factor', be very positive and motivated, and be on target to achieve your goal.

If you fail to do all of your planned activity you have two choices. The following week you must do the planned activity for that week and catch up with the activity you failed to do the previous week, or, if you don't catch up you will know you are behind target and you need to adjust your goals to take one week longer.

For example, if your goal is to give out 400 flyers every day and on Monday you only do 200, you have two choices. On Tuesday you could put out 600, or you could put out 400, but then accept you are now one day behind your goal.

This may not seem like much but if you fail to do your planned activity every week it mounts up. A goal which should have been achieved in 3 months may now take 6 months. Using a tracker means you will have no surprises. You won't reach the end of the year and wonder why you haven't achieved your goals. Your tracker will let you know, on a weekly basis, whether you are on target. If you are not, you can quickly adjust your activity to compensate and get back on track.

I have included an example of a weekly activity tracker in 'diagram 4' which you can adjust to reflect the activity you need to do on a weekly basis. At the start of each week fill in the activity you plan to do. Then, at the end of each week fill in the actual activity you achieved.

Ask yourself these questions;

Are you on target to achieve your goals?
Or, do you need to adjust what you are doing?
Are you doing enough activity?
Or, do you need to put more energy into your business?

When you track your daily activity you are checking to see if you are on course to achieve your goals every day. If you are not on track you can adjust what you need to do and tighten things up very quickly so you don't fall behind in your plan.

Diagram 4

Weekly Activity Tracker

Name:	Monday		Tuesday		Wednesday		Thursday		Friday		Saturday		Sunday		Total	
Date:	Planned	Actual	Planned	Actual	Planned	Actual	Planned	Actual	Planned	Actual	Planned	Actual	Planned	Actual	Planned	Actual
Sales per week																
Warm Market (min. 5 per day)																
Business Cards (1000 min. wk)																
Attend Training Meeting																
Personal Development																
Lead Generating Activity.																
Contact Leads per day																

Are you doing the following lead generation activities

Are you displaying your car advert?
Have you got your own press advert out?
Do you ask for referrals from every contact?
You should be able to answer **yes** to all of the above

Total personal sales for this week: ____________

Total follow up calls made: ____________

Planned leads generated: ____________

Actual leads generated: ____________

Additional necessities

Voicemail - check **3** times a day.
Follow up on leads within 24 hours.
Listen to a CD a day.
Read a book a month.
Attend all trainings.
Maintain regular contact with sponsor/upline.

Did you do the activity you planned to do this week? Yes No

Are you still on target? Yes No

Chapter 11

Your Warm Market Contact List

I have been in network marketing for many years now and I believe the contact list is the best way to build a network. In my first month I personally sponsored over 30 people from my contact list. From there I went on to build my whole organisation mainly from contact lists.

Why did I do this? Quite simply, it's the cheapest and the fastest way to build a business. It just requires a phone call.

I also believe we have a moral obligation to our family and friends to share this fantastic opportunity with them. I have shown my opportunity to all my family members. Some of them joined, some of them became customers and some led me to other people who I sponsored from the referral. When you work your list you will find some people won't join, but they will often lead you to people. Share your opportunity with everybody.

Over my years of building I've found things start to happen quickly when someone works their contact list. When you sponsor someone from an advert it takes time for the new person to trust you and feel part of the team. When you sponsor someone from your contact list, that trust is already there. You know them and they know you. The contact list is powerful because people join people they trust.

If you want to sponsor from cold market advertising, but you haven't worked your list, you are effectively saying that it's good enough for strangers, but not good enough for your friends and family. You need to look at the message you give to people. You will sponsor some people from adverts, but if you have not worked your contact list it becomes much harder. Once you have contacted everyone on your list, even if no-one joins, you will find it much easier to talk to and sponsor people through advertising.

I have a lady called Sue in my organisation who found it difficult to sponsor when she first started. She did sponsor occasionally, but she was only advertising because she didn't want to contact her friends and family. I assured her it would be much easier to sponsor from adverts if she worked her contact list first and she finally agreed to do it. Once Sue had worked her list she was amazed at how much easier she found sponsoring from adverts. Her belief in herself and her business had totally changed.

If you work your contact list, exhaust it and then advertise, you will sponsor more people from adverts because your belief and posture is very different. Once you have worked your list you are subconsciously saying to cold market prospects,

"This is an excellent business and I have shown all my friends and family."

You don't say the words but subconsciously the message will come through. The contact list is very powerful.

Become a master at working your contact list and contact everyone you know. Constantly add names to your list, don't prejudge, and teach the process. It will have a knock-on effect and the people you sponsor will copy what you do.

In my organisation we pride ourselves that the leaders have all worked their list and are well trained to teach it to their down-line. The duplication in the team is contagious.

Working your contact list can be uncomfortable to begin with, but if you don't work your list you can't teach it to your down-line and you won't get the necessary duplication. This will slow down the growth of your business.

If you feel uncomfortable contacting people you know, think about how you would feel if you attend a training or a company event and you see someone you know being recognised for an achievement, but sponsored into another team. You would not only lose out on sponsoring this person, but you will also miss out on the people they will contact through their list.

How do you think your friend, your cousin, or close associate will feel if they join with someone else? What will they think when they realise you didn't consider offering them this fantastic opportunity, or a chance to work with you? And how would they feel knowing you hadn't approached them?

You hold the key to helping other people overcome their financial problems. If you don't contact them, someone else will. It's just a matter of time. Everyone is on somebody's list, somewhere!

A few years ago I was working with someone in my team who prejudged some of the people on his list. When we got to his nephew he refused to call him because he thought he had a good job and wouldn't have the time. A while later his nephew was sponsored into the network under someone else and he is now building a big business in a different leg.

If you think the people you know wouldn't want to do what you do, imagine this. If you said to one of your successful friends, *"I'll give you £3,000 per week to sweep the road for an hour a day"*, they would say to you, *"Give me two brooms!"* just in case one breaks.

If the reason is big enough the facts don't count. This income and much more is available in this industry.

So why doesn't everybody want to use their contact list?
Many people find it uncomfortable.

Which of these two do you feel is most uncomfortable;

1. Being really broke, or
2. Telephoning the people you know?

For me, being broke is far more uncomfortable. I've been really broke, and now, thanks to my network marketing business, I'm wealthy.

Don't be embarrassed by what you are doing. Self-made, successful people in any industry or job are not embarrassed by what they do, so don't be embarrassed by what you do.

If you choose not to contact people you know, it could be you are not totally convinced network marketing will work for you, or because you have a fear of rejection. This is quite normal, but unnecessary.

If you do what you are uncomfortable doing, you will achieve results, and with these results you will lose your fear and doubt, and gain belief.

Exercise your muscle of courage!

In the next few chapters I will teach you how to draft your list, how to call people effectively, and I will give you a simple script to follow. Don't worry about making mistakes. Just get the job done. Remember, if you don't work your own list you can't teach others to work their lists.

Chapter 12

Drafting Your Warm Market Contact List

Most people only write a small list because they prejudge whether the people they know would like to join their business. When I'm working with someone who gives me a list of just twenty or thirty names I know they are only writing down the names of people they think will join their business. Contact everyone you know. Ask them to decide. Don't make the decision for them.

I was recently working with a new couple in my team. They are very motivated and worked their list extensively. While we were telephoning people on their list we contacted someone who had already been in my network marketing company for a number of years, but in a different group. This person had not had the courage to offer this new couple the opportunity and it proved to be a costly mistake for him. They have gone on to build a large business, which is growing rapidly.

Scenarios like this happen on a regular basis. Don't let it happen to you. Prejudging whether people you know would like to build a business can be very expensive.

Approach everyone, not just people who are broke and who you think need the money. Also approach those people who are wealthy.

When I was first introduced to network marketing I already had a successful conventional business with all the status symbols. I joined my network marketing company because I had no time to enjoy my money.

I have people in my organisation from many different backgrounds. Examples of occupations include successful business people, postmen, lorry drivers, city bankers, pensioners, teachers, accountants, students, shop assistants and literally people from all walks of life. Some of these people are very busy, even wealthy, however they are all looking for something their occupation can't give them, either money, time or something else.

In my early days of networking, while I was still running my conventional business full-time, I sponsored the daughter of one of my multi-millionaire clients. Although she was already wealthy she decided she needed a challenge. The team she started all those years ago through her list is still in place today. If I had prejudged my multi-millionaire client and not shown her my business, that team would never have existed.

Now you know why it is so important not to prejudge people, you need to write your list. I encourage you to have at least 200-400 contacts on your list, however just a few are better than none. To help you I have included a memory jogger in 'diagram 5'. Go through it carefully.

As you write down a name ask yourself this question.

" Who do I know that they know? "

Write down names with a contact telephone number beside them and use a mark to indicate whether you have the postal address. You need a phone number so you can cover objections on a follow-up phone call.

If you don't have a contact number for some of the people on your list, write their names down anyway because you can find a way to contact them at a later date. You can get phone numbers from directory inquiries or a mutual acquaintance, or you could post a letter or postcard asking them to get into contact with you.

I recommend you write your list in three sections, as follows, because it encourages you not to leave anyone out.

1) Make a list of people you know.

Write down all your family, friends and acquaintances.
Go through your personal address book from A - Z. If you have a party who would you invite? If you go to a party who will be there? If you get married or if you have been married who came to the wedding? Who do you work with?

These are just some ideas. I'm sure you can think of many more places where you will see people you know.

2) Make a list of people you don't know.

These are people who you don't know very well. For example; your milkman, John's friend Mary, old school or college friends, your ex-husband's or ex-wife's friends, your parents' friends or business associates in other offices. Who are the parents of your children's school friends or those they do hobbies with?

Use the memory jogger to see who you have forgotten. Put onto this list anyone you have heard of and who will have heard of you, but with whom you have very little or no contact normally. The list is endless.

3) Write a list of people who you perceive won't join.

This is your 'Chicken List.' They are people who you perceive are already wealthy because they have a high powered job or are dedicated to their job, have no time, or are owners of big houses and expensive cars, etc.

Contact everybody you have written down on your list. Beware! If you choose not to contact some of the people you know, you run the risk of these people being sponsored by someone else. It happens quite regularly.

To be completely effective your list is an on-going project. You need to continuously add names to it and then re-work your list regularly. I will cover this in a later chapter.

Diagram 5

Memory Jogger

Address book
Business cards
Christmas card list
Neighbourhood list
Mother
Father
Sisters
Brothers
Cousins
Grandparents
Uncles
Aunts
Friends
Nieces
Nephews
Grandchildren
Godparents
Godchildren
Your friends
Your parents' friends
In-laws
Step-children
Parents' neighbours
College friends
Work colleagues
Your neighbours
Your boss
Former neighbours
Children's friend's parents

Who do you know who is an;
Accountant
Actor / actress
Agriculturalist
Air hostess / steward
Antique dealer
Armed forces
Art instructor
Association member
Attorney
Bank clerk
Banker
Barber
Bar worker
Beautician
Bookmaker
Builder
Bus driver
Carpet layer
Car salesman
Care worker
Carpenter
Chef
Childcare provider
Chiropractor
Coach
Communication worker
Cook
Dance teacher
Dancer
Decorator
Delivery driver
Dentist
Dietician
Doctor
Dressmaker
Dry cleaner
Editor
Electrician
Emergency medical staff
Engineer
Ex-army
Farmer
Fast food employee
Fireman
Fisherman
Florist
Funeral director
Furniture salesman
Gardener
Gas station attendant
Hairdresser
Hotel manager
Housekeeper
Hunter
Insurance agent
Insurance sales rep
Jeweller
Judge
Lab technician
Landscaper
Lawyer
Legal secretary / assistant
Librarian
Life Insurance sales person
Lifeguard
Machine shop worker
Maintenance engineer
Manager
Market stall worker
Martial arts instructor
Mechanic
Model
Motel owner
Music teacher
Nurse
Odd job man
Optician
Painter
Paperboy
Pharmacist
Pilot
Policeman
Postman
Preacher
Printer
Property manager
Restaurant owner
Retail sales clerk
Retired co-worker
Rotary Club
Sailor
Sales rep
School principal or head teacher
Scuba instructor
Secretary
Security guard
Sheriff
Shop owner
Social worker
Soldier
Stay-at-home parent
Stewardess
Student
Tailor
Taxi driver
Teacher
Traffic warden
Truck driver
Tupperware rep
Vicar
Waiter / waitress
Wedding photographer
Welder

Ask yourself these Questions

Who is dissatisfied?
Who is motivated by money?
Who is successful?
Who works in restaurants?
Who is not working?
Who is unemployed?
Who has done MLM before?
Who has lots of time?
Who likes personal development?
Who does your taxes?
Who works in a bank?
Who is their own boss?
Who are your friends?
Who did you go to school with?
Who wants more freedom?
Who works with children?
Who do you respect?
Who likes to dance?
Who wants a holiday?
Who walks their dog with you?
Who needs a new car?
Who is self motivated?
Who is on your wedding list?
Who do you dislike?
Who likes to play team sports?
Who is disabled?
Who wants a promotion?
Who sold you your car?
Who goes to church?
Who do you do business with?
Who lives across the street?
Who has lots of parties?
Who is ambitious?
Who is a high achiever?
Who has blond hair?
Who works with computers?
Who likes a challenge?

Who did you meet on a plane?
Who have you helped?
Who builds web sites?
Who is attractive?
Who is bald?
Who plays football?
Who are your goods suppliers?
Who has a new computer?
Who wears hats?
Who does the same hobbies?
Who likes gardening?
Who drives a Jaguar?
Who drives a posh car?
Who has lived abroad?
Who works where you eat out?
Who likes to learn new things?
Who wants more for their family?
Who likes to work for themselves?
Who is short?
Do you know any twins?
Who did you meet on holiday?
Who is tall?
Who is retired?
Who is a single dad / mum?
Who did you grow up with?
Who is teachable?
Who goes to the health club/gym?
Who helps charities?
Who wants to retire early?
Who tells jokes?
Who works nights?
Who works weekends?
Who is a workaholic?
Who quit smoking?
Who smokes?
Who has recently been promoted?
Who has red hair?

Who uses the bus?
Who has just had a baby?
Who did you see at school reunion?
Who was at your college reunion?
Who is popular?
Who likes to camp?
Who has just got married?
Who is in debt?
Who has been on holiday?
Who is on a diet?
Who is outgoing?
Who drives a Ford?
Who is a natural leader?
Who has a high voice?
Who would you invite to a party?
Who lives on the corner?
Who drives a Chevy?
Who drives an old car?
Who has a pick up truck?
Who is on a debate team?
Who is sporty?
Who has office skills?
Who is very confident?
Who is divorced?
Who likes to help people?
Who likes the internet?
Who plays baseball?
Who has a deep voice?
Who works in a shop?
Who is on your Xmas card list?
Who owns a small business?
Who is in your school photo?
Who sings in a choir?
Who has dark hair?
Who is in college?
Who has a boat?
Who repairs your house?
Who plays basketball?
Who does fundraising?
Who will help you?
Who likes to buy things?
Who has your phone number?
Who recycles?
Who likes to talk on the phone?
Who are your customers?
Who bought a new home?
Who bought a new car?
Who has lots of energy?
Who has a lovely smile?
Who needs an extra income?
Who has a part-time job?
Who works nights?
Who needs more time?
Who looks up to you?
Who has expensive tastes?
Who did you meet at a party?
Who is always busy?
Who wears glasses?
Who dresses very well?
Who is unhappy with income?
Who is goal orientated?
Who has a moustache?
Who watches TV often?
Who plays an instrument?
Who is positive?
Who drives a Porsche?
Who has public speaking skills?
Who has a dangerous job?
Who has organisational skills?
Who uses the train?

Chapter 13

Working Your Contact List

I recommend you always work in pairs when you telephone people on your list. Many people find it uncomfortable asking those they know if they would like to see information on their business. Working together makes the telephone less of a challenge and you are more likely to finish the task or goal you set for yourself. You will also spend less time on personal conversation when you have someone else with you in the room or on three-way telephone calling.

Don't wait to contact people on your list until you are earning a higher income. A part-time income of £100-£300 per month is very relatable. Think about it. Many people don't have £100-£300 per month as a disposable income for luxuries such as dinner out, going to the cinema, a bottle of wine or holidays. I very seldom tell prospects what I'm earning. I always tell them the incomes and testimonials of other distributors who have recently joined. Most people relate to these stories.

When you're talking to your contacts on the phone be enthusiastic and positive about your business, but not over the top. Avoid getting drawn into a long personal conversation.

People you know may want to have a lengthy chat, so tell them it's a business call and you will call them back at a later date for a longer social chat. It's important to use your time effectively.

Allocate yourself a period of time to make phone calls each day, usually between about 6 and 9 in the evening. During this time you need to call as many people as you can from your list. Saturday and Sunday after 10 am are also good times to work your list as many people are at home.

The aim of the first telephone call to people on your contact list is to get them to agree to attend a house meeting, meet for a coffee so you can show them your opportunity, or post them an information pack or DVD. You need them to see the big picture and make an informed choice about whether they want to join your opportunity after seeing information.

Don't get drawn into a lengthy conversation about your business in this call. Get them to agree to meet with you or to receive information and then politely end the call. I always say,

"It will take me an hour to tell you or 15 minutes to show you. Let me send the info / show you at my house."

You need to monitor your success in getting your contacts to agree to attend your house meeting, meet up with you, or to receive an information pack. For every 10 calls you make from your list, at least 6, and in some cases all 10 of the people you call, will accept information or agree to attend your house meeting. This ratio is achieved because the way the phone call is done is non-threatening.

If you make 10 calls and only 2 accept then STOP. You are doing something wrong! Don't carry on. You are blowing people out before getting information to them. Refer to the script in 'diagram 6' and check you are following it. Make sure you are positive and enthusiastic when you are speaking to people on the telephone.

If someone can't attend your house meeting, or they live too far away, make sure you arrange to meet up at a later date or post them an information pack.

All information you give to prospects must have your name and phone number on it. The following example demonstrates why.

A colleague of mine joined the business because he was passed a DVD from his sister. She got it from someone she bumped into in a bar, and it was left lying around for months before being watched. If there had been no label on it he would probably have joined with a different distributor. Label everything. Don't lose any prospects.

When you send a DVD or CD ROM always send it without highlighting the company name. This is because people, like myself, may prejudge the company in the beginning. Just label it with your name and contact details.

If you send information via e-mail or a website, always post a written information pack or DVD, as well. You can follow-up information sent by e-mail very quickly, however, it's often only partly read and is easily deleted. Hard copy information can be kept or passed on in the future, or even retrieved from the bin if someone wishes they had given your opportunity a better look.

A few years ago I had a dustman sign into my team. The person the information pack had originally been sent to wasn't interested and threw it in the bin. The dustman found it and signed into the business. Using a computer is fast and effective but always post an information pack as well.

All the people who say 'no' to receiving information or 'no' to your opportunity, either on the telephone, at an interview or at a house meeting, are people you can ask for referrals. See the chapter on referrals further on in this book. Even if you don't sponsor a particular person from your list you are often able to get referrals from friends and family. Remember, if you don't ask, you don't get!

Chapter 14

Scripts for Working Your Contact List

When you contact people on your list always use a script. 'Diagram 6' is an example of the very successful script I give to people I work with in my organisation. Don't worry if you make a mess of the first few phone calls. It really doesn't matter. Get started and get the job done. Don't be someone who spends hours analysing and perfecting a plan but then doesn't put it into action. It is better to do it wrong than never to do it at all, and you will be learning by your errors.

I have included two brief conversations below, to demonstrate how your telephone calls may go.

"Hi John, it's Mary. How are you doing? How's the family? This is just a quick call. I've just got involved in a business. I've only been doing it for a few weeks and I've earned £200 profit. It's going really well and I'm expanding into your area. I'd like to tell you about it. Can we meet up for coffee?"

The person will generally say, *"Yes. What is it?"*
"I knew you would be interested. Come to my house on Tuesday and I'll tell you about it."

Alternatively ; *"Hi Ben, it's George. Are you aware that I've recently become involved in a business? I've been doing it for two weeks now and I'm very excited about it. Can I send you some free information without obligation?"*

Diagram 6

Script For List

Contacting Family / Friends

60 second pleasantries
ie; House, Family, Pets, Work, etc

Reason For Call
Just started my own business
Going very well
Very excited about it

Income / Turnover
(If you want to tell them how much
you have earned in the last week / month)

Expanding my business
ie; expanding in your area

Free Information without obligation

If local invite to house meeting

If distance, post DVD or information pack

Re-contacting people you have already told about your opportunity

Once you have been involved in your networking business for a while, you may find you have already spoken to everyone on your list and many people didn't join for varying reasons. When you first approached them you may have messed up the telephone call by giving them badly phrased details or simply too much information. You could have told them about your opportunity rather than showing them. If you told them the name of your network marketing company they may have prejudged your opportunity before seeing the big picture. The company name is not a secret, but people often prejudge companies they have heard of. You may not have been able to inform them about your company effectively.

However badly you contacted people the first time you must keep re-contacting everybody on your list every 3-6 months.

Telephoning is the best way to re-contact people. Many distributors in my organisation have used the following example with great success and you may choose to use it when talking to your contacts.

"Hello John, do you remember I showed you my business some time ago? I must apologise to you because I didn't do it justice. I didn't show you the full picture. I've been involved for 12 months now and it's going really well. Would you mind if I send you some free information, without obligation, so you can evaluate it properly for yourself?
If it isn't for you, you may know someone who would be interested. Many thanks."

Other ways to re-contact people on your warm list include sending people a copy of your cheque or proof of income, any positive press, newsletters, or let them know how the extra income you are earning is helping you, etc.

Christmas is always a good time to re-contact your warm market. When you send Christmas cards to your family and friends include a copy of your recent earnings or an information pack. Remind them that you have a part-time network marketing business. Then, in the New Year give them a call and follow-up. Ask if they would be interested in finding out more information on your business, or do they know anyone who would like some information? Just ask the question. If you don't ask, you don't get.

You have to stay in touch with people on your contact list until the timing is right for them to join your business. One distributor in my organisation kept in touch with a person on their contact list for over 4 years. Once the timing was right for them they joined and built a very large business.

Re-contacting people about a new network

If you have been in one or more networks before, you may feel that anyone you tell about your current opportunity is bound to say 'no' because you have spoken to them a few times about different businesses or opportunities. You can use wording like this;

"Hello Jack, do you remember I showed you / you got involved in my network marketing business when I was doing .... I'm so pleased you didn't join / left as it didn't work for me. I've been involved with another company for a while now and it's going very well. I didn't want to contact you earlier because I wanted to make sure this one works."

Explain how the extra income you are earning is helping you or changing your lifestyle.

"Can I send you some free information, without obligation, so you can evaluate it for yourself? Please keep an open mind. If it's not for you, you may know someone. Many thanks."

Re-contacting people who don't want to do network marketing

You may also have contacted people in the past who said they don't want to do networking. I can recommend this approach;

"Hello Mary, do you remember I spoke to you about a network marketing company, ..., in the past, and you said it wasn't for you and you didn't want to do a network? I wonder if you can help me. Do you know anyone who has been involved in networking, perhaps friends, family, acquaintances, or friends of friends, as I'm still involved with the same network and it's going very well."

Explain how the extra income you are earning is helping you or changing your lifestyle.

"How are things going for you at the moment?
Would you consider taking another look at my business?
If it's for you, great, if it isn't for you, that's great, too, as I know you probably won't want to do it."

The reason you mention, towards the end that they won't want to do it, is because you're taking the opportunity away from them and most people don't like having things taken away.

Contacting people by post

The quickest way to work your list is for you to take the plunge and get on the telephone. However, if there are people on your list who you simply refuse to contact by phone, you could post a letter, information or a DVD.

I don't recommend this approach because it isn't as effective as using the telephone. However, it's better everyone knows you are involved in the opportunity, so if they are interested they will join with you.

The accompanying letter should ask them to contact you if they would like to discuss the opportunity further. Or you can use a third party letter;

"Dear Jack,
Please can you help me? I have just started a new business and I was wondering if you knew anyone who may be interested? I have enclosed some information. Please pass it on if anyone comes to mind. Many thanks, James."

Chapter 15

Running a House Meeting

House meetings are a major leverage of your time because you show your opportunity to many people at the same time. The key to a successful house meeting is in setting it up correctly and over my years in network marketing I've found the method I'm about to teach you is the best way to set it up.

Your house meeting won't be a success if you don't invite people effectively. You can blow people out by telling them too much information over the phone or by being too pushy.

They may say, *"Yes, I will come,"* just to get you off the phone but then not turn up.

Before you start making your phone calls choose two days in the following week when you will run your house meetings. Invite each person to one and, if they can't attend, then invite them to the other.

Invite each person as an individual. Talk to them as though they are the only person invited. They don't need to know there will also be other people attending. If you tell them it's a meeting some people may not turn up.

Once people arrive at your house meeting it's not a problem. Say to them, *"I hope you don't mind, I've asked a few other people to come as well to save a bit of time."*

You need to aim for at least twenty people / couples accepting to come to your house meeting. Out of these you will on average sponsor four or five distributorships. Therefore, if you do two house meetings a week you could sponsor ten people a week. This is a massive leverage of your time.

If you are having a large house meeting you may consider asking your active up-line to attend to assist you or, alternatively, you could ask them to do a 10 minute conference call after your presentation or DVD.

On the day of your house meeting, set everything up before people start to arrive. Have your opportunity presenter ready, or put the DVD in the machine ready to go.

Once people are seated give a brief testimony. Tell them how long you've been involved, whether you are full-time or part-time in your business and why you started. For example, you are fed up with your job or you need more money. Explain how much you are earning and how the extra income is helping you. After the testimony, say there is a short DVD or presentation and suggest to them that they keep questions to the end. If people interrupt with questions during your presentation / DVD, say you will answer them later on.

If you are running your house meeting with a DVD, watch it yourself even if you have seen it a thousand times already. Focus on the television. If you don't you will be inviting people to ask questions and ruin it for everybody else.

You want them to focus on the information. If someone asks you a question you should whisper,
"*I'll cover it at the end. Thanks very much.*"

Try to sit towards the back, preferably in a corner, so no-one can make eye contact with you. Slowly look round the room to see what people are doing.

If someone is sitting on the edge of their seat and their posture and body language is positive, make a mental note that you need to talk to them at the end. If you are giving a presentation at the front of the room watch for these signs while you are talking.

Some people will be fascinated by the ceiling for the entire house meeting! This is normal and it doesn't matter. They are telling you they are not interested at this time.

Following a DVD, you must turn off the television before continuing. Once your DVD or presentation has finished, show proof of your monthly income or cheque and that of your attending up-line, if you can. Remember, a small income of £100 or £300 a month is a very powerful success story because it's relatable. It is in addition to a normal full-time income and can be a life-line for some people.

Show any positive press releases of your opportunity or the networking industry. Very quickly and very briefly, right at the end, you should demonstrate some products or show product information. If you have product information such as a catalogue, open it up halfway through to show the range of products and not just the front cover.

To end the presentation stand up and ask, *"Does anyone have any questions?"* Some people fire questions and some don't.

Finally ask, "*When would you all like to start?* "
It sounds really cheeky, but it gets a smile out of most people. It's effective and it gives you the opportunity to cover more objections.

After you have finished your presentation to the group, talk to some people individually. Focus on the keenest first. You should already have one or two people earmarked as interested. If you have up-line at your house meeting to help you, take two each. Sit down and spend time with them, covering objections. Once you have dealt with your two key prospects talk to the other people in the room.

You should have sponsoring packs at your house meeting. This is really important as you can sign the paperwork with people who want to join, right there and then. Remember to leverage your time. If four people want to join and you have four sponsoring packs, talk them through filling in the paperwork all together. Go through your normal 'start up' routine with the new sign-ups.

If you run out of sponsoring packs, which often happens at house meetings, take payment immediately and sign them in as soon as you can.

You will find that some people who attend your house meeting are not at all interested in your opportunity, and there will be others who are interested but not yet ready to join. Send them home with information. Often people read it and after a period of time either join or pass it on to other people.

Make sure you ask everyone at the house meeting for referrals and find out if they are interested in becoming a customer.

If a person said they would come to your house meeting but then fails to turn up, give them a quick call the next day.

"Hi Peter, where were you last night?
.......Not to worry, can you come on Friday / Can you come tomorrow? "

And if they can't come say to them,
"I'll tell you what I'll do. I'll put a DVD / information pack in the post to you. Can I have it back in a couple of days please?"

Some people can't come for genuine reasons, so do offer them information and give them a call two days later to follow-up. Ask them if they received the information pack in the post, have they watched it / read it, cover any questions / objections and then ask if they would like to join.

If they say,
"No" reply,
"May I ask why?" to see if they have an objection or query which you can cover.

I have included a chapter on covering objections later in the book and a 'follow-up flow chart' in 'diagram 7' to help you when you are following up on information packs which you have given out. I recommend you always have the follow-up flow chart in front of you when you do your follow-ups. It will remind you to ask for referrals and cover objections.

If you contact 50 - 100 people a week from your contact list your first few weeks of sponsoring will be organised chaos.

You will make loads of telephone calls, run lots of house meetings and the momentum in your team will be unstoppable.

Follow this formula and in a month you should have two or more powerful legs and an organisation which is ready to explode.

Chapter 16

Referrals

I want to show you the power of referrals with a story which happened to a couple in my organisation. They went to a wedding and were talking to a friend who wasn't interested, but the friend said they knew someone who they thought would be. That person was sponsored into their team and built a large business. The up-line now make a great income simply because they asked for referrals.

Asking for a referral is asking someone if they can recommend anyone who would like to see information. Referrals are new contacts with no financial cost to you.

Don't just ask people if they can recommend anyone. Many people will say "*No!*" Help them. Ask them questions. Many people will help you if you ask. Here are some suggestions;

"Do you know anybody who has got their own business?"

"Do you know anyone who has been involved in the network marketing industry in the past?"

"Do you know anyone who requires an extra income?"

"Would an extra £100 to £500 a month help someone you know?"

"Can you refer me to someone who would like some information?"

For example;

"Do you know anyone who is successful, who has recently been made redundant, who requires a part-time income or who has been involved in the networking industry in the past?"

"Yes? Great! What's their name please? What's their number?"

If you say,
"Do you mind if I give them a call?"
you are immediately asking the person if they mind. Keep it very positive.

"Yes I know someone who always wants to earn more money!"

"Fantastic, what's their name please? John.....what's John's number please?"

You may feel it's a bit cheeky but it works really well and I've sponsored many distributors from referrals in this way.

Chapter 17

Helping Your Down-line To Work Their Contact List

I was recently working with a lady in my team who was very, very nervous about calling people she knew prior to working with me on her list. On the day of the appointment to build, she was so nervous she initially refused to pick up the telephone. However, within 10 minutes of starting to call people she was making all the calls herself.

How did I do this?

I encouraged her to pick up the phone and make the first call. I told her to follow the script (see diagram 6), to be herself and said it didn't matter if she messed it up. In fact, I actually encouraged her not to get it totally correct. To make her feel comfortable I said to her,

"Show me how wrong you can get it."

I was not putting her under any pressure to get the call correct and it gave her confidence to make it.

At the end of the first call, even though it went very well, I again encouraged her to make errors on the next one. After five calls she was up and running and feeling very confident.

If you want your business to grow quickly you need to make it happen. Very few people will actually go to you and ask for your help. Encourage your team to work their contact lists by talking to each of your down-line individually and if they want your help, book individual appointments to work with them.

If the person in your down-line lives more than half an hour away from you, you can still work together very effectively, using three-way or mini-conference calling. I like using three-way telephone calling when helping people to work their contact lists because it is very time efficient. I can book people into hourly slots and help several down-line in one evening.

The day before you use three-way calling to help someone to work their list, ask them to post, fax or e-mail to you just the names and phone numbers of their contacts and to number each one, 1, 2, 3, etc. Arrange for them to telephone you at an agreed time on the evening of the 'Appointment to Build'. Once they ring you, you then use the three-way call facility on your telephone to connect with the contacts on their list.

Listen to them make each call and take the opportunity to coach them in-between. Make sure they stick to the script and keep the phone call short. They should not spend too long on personal conversation or divulge too much information about your network marketing company because they need to let the information pack or house meeting do the work.

If you are working with someone in your down-line who is very uncomfortable with the idea of calling people on their contact list, or they are simply too terrified to pick up the telephone to make that first phone call, you may choose to take a more active role in helping them. Once they have drafted their list use three-way calling to speak to the first person on their list yourself. The conversation should go something like this;

"Hello, can I speak to James please?"

"Hello James, my name is John. How are you?"

"I'm calling on behalf of Peter Smith. I don't know if you are aware but Peter has recently become involved in his own business. Peter and I are working closely together and Peter is doing extremely well. The reason for this call is to see if you're interested in receiving some free information as we're expanding into your area.

Of course, there's no obligation.

I'll ask Peter to post you an information pack.

It's been a pleasure talking to you. Let me pass you to Peter."

At the end of the call Peter must get onto the phone just to say a few words.

"John's working with me to help me build my business. It's all going very well and I'm looking forward to speaking to you again soon."

After only a couple of calls, using this approach, your down-line will realise how easy it is and be making the calls himself.

If you are working a list on the telephone with someone who is very confident you still need to be involved in the initial telephone calls. Make sure they are following the script (see diagram 6), not spending too much time on the phone and that they are successful in getting people to agree to receive an information pack or attend their house meeting. You need to remember, the key to a successful house meeting is in getting people to attend it. You don't need to be too involved with the calls. Just sit in the same room, coach them briefly and check they are inviting their contacts effectively.

You can continue to assist your down-line when they have their house meeting. If they live very local to you (within half an hour), or they are having a house meeting with more than ten potential distributorships attending, then you may choose to attend the house meeting to assist them.

If you live too far away to actually attend their house meeting you can still be very effective in helping your down-line. After the initial presentation ask them to call you and do a ten minute loud speaker telephone call. Give a testimony and answer questions.

By leveraging your time like this you are letting your down-line and the people attending their house meeting know it is possible to build a big business, on a very part-time basis, and to be time effective while doing it. It gives people the message that anyone can build a business.

Chapter 18

No List, No Money!

Some distributors are not prepared to contact people from their warm market, or they think they don't know anyone and they have no money for advertising. In other words, they have no list and no money! Initially, it may be more of a challenge to build a business like this, but if the desire is there it's not impossible.

One of the ways to overcome the money situation is, of course, to sponsor people who will contribute to your monthly turnover. Contacting people you know is the best way to start sponsoring. Everybody knows some people, you may just think you don't! You have neighbours where you live, people you buy from when you go shopping, and if you have children you know the parents of their school friends. You have a postman, dustbin men and work colleagues. The list is endless. A warm market contact list is not just comprised of people you know really well. It's also people who you have contact with and know a little bit or, sometimes, may just have heard of. Refer to the memory jogger in 'diagram 5'.

Some people are simply not prepared to work a traditional list when they first join a network marketing company. They don't have belief in the company or in themselves yet. There are other ways to build a team and the alternative is using cold market advertising, however these activities cost varying amounts of money.

Common cold market advertising activities include;

- Advertising in newspapers which can be very expensive but requires no labour,

- Handing out fliers and business cards which cost money for the printing and paper,

- Putting cards or posters in shop windows which you usually have to pay for per week.

There are also many other lead generating tools.

Generally the more time efficient a method of generating leads is, the more it costs. Balance the money you spend on advertising with the time you have available to build your business.

Generating leads with no list, no money!

There are also many ways to get cold market contact leads without spending a lot of money. I'll go through some of these with you now.

Once you have been in a network marketing company for a few weeks and have some customers, they become part of your warm market. Talk to your customers and build up a rapport. Tell them how your business is going and ask if they know anyone who needs an extra income.

Every time you sell a product, put a slip into the bag explaining that you are looking for new people, and do they know anyone who would like to see some information. Make sure it will get the customer's attention. It can be typed or handwritten, and it must have your name and contact details on it so the customer will contact you and not the company.

Create signs to put in your car. Use your car as a mobile advertising board. As you are driving around it will be seen by lots of people. Also, put a sign in the front windows of your house and / or your garden. Anyone coming to your front door or walking down your street will see it.

When you are invited to parties, coffee mornings or social events, make sure everyone around you knows you have a part-time business and you are looking for people who would like to look at information or earn an extra income.

Always carry business cards to give out to prospects. If you don't have business cards, use slips of paper with your contact details on. Also keep a notepad and pen to write down the contact details of people who want to see information on your business.

Put a link on the bottom of all e-mails you send, so people can go directly to your website, or add a signature to your e-mails asking if recipients would like to see information on your business.

When you get junk mail and circulars in the post they often come with a pre-paid envelope. Post back a flier, a business card, a handwritten slip of paper or any information from your company with your contact details on. It costs you nothing to send the envelope back to them.

Newsagents often let you pay to put a shop card in their window. However many shops local to you, like a village butcher, would allow you to put a shop card or poster in their window free of charge, especially if you are a regular. Ask all your local shops.

Search the 'work wanted' section of any free papers or daily papers you receive. Although people won't specifically be looking for network marketing, you can still ring them up and offer them information on your opportunity. Do the same on internet sites with people who are looking for a job.

Become a master of the 'three foot rule'. Talk to anyone who is within three foot of you everywhere you go. For example, in the supermarket queue, bank queue, your milkman, delivery drivers or people you meet walking down the street. There are thousands of times when you will be standing next to people for a short period of time. If you overhear someone moaning about not having enough money, lack of time, needing a holiday, or car breaking down, interrupt them. Strike up a conversation. Tell them you know a way to help and would they like some free information. Say it is paying for your shopping, bought you a new car, or it is paying for your holiday. Let them know how the extra income has helped you.

Speak to people who do street surveys. When they ask you questions turn it around. You are giving them your time, how about they give you some of theirs! Ask how much they get paid for doing it, do they like doing it and do they want some free information on what you do?

You can also do a street survey yourself. Look professional. Get a clip board and pen and ask people some questions.

Do you like the car you drive?
What is your dream holiday location?
Do you like your job?
Do you get paid enough?

Stand outside a train station, a bus station, or on a busy high street. Ask people for their name and phone number and give them an information pack to take home.

When you get telephone sales calls for double glazing or mobile phones, etc, don't just hang up. They phoned you. It's not costing you anything so ask them whether they enjoy their job. Are they well paid? Talk to them. Ask if they want free information or to look at your web site.

When you get religious callers or sales reps knocking on your door, ask them in and show them a DVD, or take their contact details and give them some information to take away with them.

All these ideas work and they are very cheap or totally free of charge. Just be confident. Ask yourself what you are prepared to do to build your business.

You can also save money by using your current sales aids more effectively. For example, show people your products more quickly, in half an hour instead of an hour, or more frequently, demonstrate the products five times a week instead of twice a week.

You can earn more money by selling more products. If you need money to purchase tools to build your business sell more products and re-invest the money. Most network marketing companies have no limit to the volume of products a distributor can sell in any one month. Therefore, if you need a massive income for a short period of time it's available for you to earn.

However, this is a job scenario. If you work more, you earn more and if you work less, you earn less. I recommend your business is well balanced between selling products, sponsoring people and teaching your team. By doing this you will, eventually, totally own your life.

Chapter 19

How to Sponsor Effectively from Adverts

Cold market leads can be generated in many ways and you can receive a prospect's details by one of several mediums; through the post, on e-mail, via a website, by text or by telephone.

How you receive a lead can influence the way you send information about your opportunity back to them. If you receive a lead via your web site or e-mail it's likely you will send them information in the form of a link to your web site or a PDF.

If your adverts have a phone number for prospects to ring, answering their call can be dealt with in several different ways.

The first is to use your home phone or a dedicated number and answer it immediately every time it rings. This method ensures speed. However, the phone call may interrupt you at inconvenient times, for example, when you are busy or at three o'clock in the morning! It means you can never totally focus on other things, or relax when you want to. You are always on call!

You could also have a dedicated line with a permanent 24 hour answerphone. This is definitely a better option than answering every phone call immediately.

It would have a script specific to your business, such as;

"Thank you for responding to the advert. Please speak slowly and clearly, giving your full name, address, spelling any unusual words, a full post code and a non-mobile number and a free information pack will be sent to you in the post. Please note, info packs will not be sent without a contact number, and please can you inform us where you saw the advert."

This works really well and most people do leave a contact number. You mention 'non-mobile' because it's cheaper to call a land-line than a mobile phone. Very importantly, if they don't leave a phone number please DO still send the information pack. The prospect may have forgotten to leave a telephone number and some people will call you to join your team once they have seen the information.

If you use a system where you set up appointments or interviews, your telephone script would be similar, but say, *"....and we will get back to you as soon as possible."*

When you advertise for cold market contacts you need to respond quickly because people reply to multiple adverts, not just yours. If you are too slow your prospects could be sponsored by somebody else, possibly even before you contact them.

Your third option is a voicemail communications system. This acts just like an answerphone and it is also an essential all-round business tool. It does everything an answerphone does, with the added advantage that you can access your voicemail from anywhere, enabling you to contact prospects very quickly.

Once you start to build a team there are many other benefits. Without voicemail, if you want to pass an advertising lead to a down-line you need to laboriously write the details down, then either e-mail or phone your down-line and recite the details. When you use voicemail it takes just seconds to press a button and copy the entire message over to them.

If you have a team of 50 people it would take you hours to stay in contact with everybody using individual phone calls and your message could change if you ask your front-line people to pass messages to their down-line.

With voicemail you can communicate with everyone in your team very time efficiently. You can leave a short one or two minute message, to a specific person in your team, which they will pick up next time they check their voicemail. They can then answer you in an equally time efficient manner.

You are also able to leave group broadcasts. You can send the same message to everyone in your team at the same time.

For example,
"Hello everyone, I hope you are all well! This is a reminder that we have our group training on Saturday at the City Inn Hotel, starting promptly at 2pm. Please make sure you introduce any new prospects to me so I can say hello. I also have a fabulous story at the end of this message, here goes, hold the line, ..."

At the end of this message you can then copy across a story from the original person who left it. It could be a motivational story from a new distributor, just a month into their business, who has achieved wonderful sales and sponsored a couple of people from their warm market contact list.

Operating a voicemail communication system within your business is very time efficient and means you keep good communication lines open with everybody in your team, even those who are very new.

I believe a voicemail communication system is essential if you want to build a big business. As long as it is used properly it is a very powerful business tool. To be completely effective you need to check your voicemail at least three times a day and you need to teach your team to duplicate you.

Chapter 20

Appointments and Interviews

Once a prospect leaves their contact details on your voicemail or answerphone you can contact them in one of several different ways.

One method is to telephone each prospect, tell them a bit about your business and invite them to an interview or set up an appointment. You should keep your conversation as short as possible, bearing in mind your objective is to get them to agree to attend an appointment or an interview so you can show them your opportunity in person.

Your conversation may be similar to this;

"Hello John,
You responded to an advert to earn an extra income.
May I ask, are you looking for part-time or full-time work?
Are you working at the moment?
What income are you looking for?
Would you have 8-12 hours per week?
Great, it sounds like you could be one of the people I'm looking for! We need to book an appointment to get together."

If your prospect asks what they have to do you could respond with;

"I'm expanding my business into your area and I'm looking for several different types of people to work with including retailers and team leaders. You'll be working from home with flexible hours to suit you and full training and support will be given once you get started. Would this interest you?"

"Great, let's set up an interview. Can you meet me at .... I'm available tomorrow lunchtime at 1pm, or Thursday evening at 7:30pm. Which one would suit you?"

Giving specific times allows you to maintain control of the conversation. If they can't make either time, be flexible, but remain in control.

You have options as to where you hold the interview. The most time efficient option for you would be to hold hourly 'interviews' at your own home or office. You have no travelling and if a prospect is late or does not arrive then you can catch up with other things.

Your next best option is a neutral place of your choosing where you can see people in hourly appointment slots, for example, in the reception of a hotel or any quiet place known to you. Make sure you have something with you to do in case you get a no-show. Carry a self-development book, or write your planner for the following week, etc.

You could also choose to hold the interview at the home of your prospect. However, this is the least time efficient option because you need to add adequate travelling time and also pay for the cost of your fuel. If you choose this option, make sure you call your prospect 30 minutes before your appointment time to confirm the appointment.

When making appointments it's important to fill your diary. If possible, book appointments to follow one after the other and try to avoid big gaps in-between. This will use your time most efficiently. If you do find you have 'dead time' between appointments don't waste it. Fill it with lead generating or business building activity.

During the appointment, you need to remember you are showing your prospect how great your opportunity is, not twisting their arm and talking them into joining. Don't pressurise people. If you persuade them to join the business you will always need to persuade them to stay in the business. Give them the information and let them decide for themselves.

If your attitude is wrong you may come across as being desperate to get people into your team. This works in reverse. A prospect may receive the message you need them in your business to make money off them.

If you think you are doing this, adjust your attitude and posture. When you introduce someone into your business have the philosophy that they are starting their own business for themselves. You have a great opportunity and you don't need them, they need you.

At the end of the appointment or interview you must ask when they would like to get started. Many people feel too uncomfortable to 'close' a conversation with a prospect effectively. However, this isn't being 'pushy', it's taking charge of the situation. It gives your prospect confidence that you can help them to change their financial situation.

If you find you are talking to a lot of people who are very interested in your opportunity, but you are not sponsoring anyone, it is possible that you are not 'closing' your interviews effectively by asking the question, *"When do you want to join?"*

The ability to 'close' effectively is essential whether the prospect is someone from your warm list or responding to an advert. However, if you feel uncomfortable when you first start asking this question, practice on people you don't know, from cold market advertising. After the interview or appointment you are unlikely to see them again, unless they join your business. Just be confident. If you don't feel confident, try to appear confident and the confidence will come.

You can ask people when they would like to join in many different ways. Choose one or two which you are most comfortable with and practice asking the question. If you find it really uncomfortable, try asking it to yourself in front of a mirror. Smile and be natural.

"When can I get you started?"
"When would you like to join my business?"
"When do you want to start?"
"When would you like to start your own business?"
"When would you like to join?"
"Great, let's get you started!"

Your prospect will reply with something similar to one of these;

"Urrr, no......., it's a great opportunity, but it's not for me!"
Ask "*Why not?*" Cover objections, ask the question again and if the answer is still "no" ask for referrals and end the interview / appointment.

"No, I'm not sure about ...."
Ask if it's the only reason, cover all objections, ask the question again and if the answer is still 'no' ask for referrals and end the interview / appointment.

"I may be interested in the future, but right now I don't have the time ......"
Once again, cover objections, ask the question again and if the answer is still 'no' ask for referrals and then end the interview / appointment.

Remember, if your prospect says 'no' to joining your opportunity, phone them one or two days later to do a follow-up. See if they have any other concerns or they have changed their mind. Unless thay are adamantly saying 'no', ask when they would like to join again, and ask for referrals.

Or they may say,
"Yes, I think I would like to do this. What do I do next?"

Don't be surprised. People do want to join your business. You did! You should already have talked about a start-up cost or fee during the interview. **Keep smiling and reply**,

"Great, how would you like to pay?"
or *"Do you have a credit card?"*

Remember, keep it simple. Don't start talking too much at this point. They already want to join your business, don't talk them out of it.

Chapter 21

Information by Post and Follow-Up Messages

Many people choose to post an information pack either in a written format or a DVD. If you choose this route there are several things you have to do. The information pack must be posted 1st class, the same day you receive the lead. Your contact details must be on every piece of literature, including the DVD, and you should enclose a very short covering letter. You don't need to repeat any information included in the information pack so it should read like this;

"Dear Simon, please find enclosed the information pack as requested. If you have any further questions please do not hesitate to contact me. Regards, Peter"

It is very short and simple. In my years of building, I've found the more information you include in your covering letter, the less likely it is your prospect will look at or read the information pack. It's just a courtesy letter. Always ask them to call you as you are demonstrating the correct posture. Of course, it's important you ring them to follow-up if they don't call you.

One to two days after sending your information pack to a prospect you must telephone them to follow-up. I recommend you use a follow-up flow chart. Keep it in front of you and refer to it with each telephone call you make. I have included the flow chart I use with my team, in 'diagram 7' for you to use. Answer any questions the prospect has and then 'close' the conversation effectively. Ask the question *"When would you like to start?"*

The format for asking this question is the same as for appointments, you just ask the question on the phone rather than in person and you respond to the reply in the same way.

You don't have to be a sales person or even very good on the phone to use this method. Posting an information pack and following-up using a flow chart is very duplicatable when you are building your team.

I recommend you have your own website and an on-line information pack which you can send to prospects who respond via e-mail. It's possible to follow-up an information pack in PDF format within one hour.

I sponsored a person like this recently. I sent him an information pack in PDF format and called him one hour later to follow-up. The conversation went like this;

"Have you received the information pack on e-mail?"
"No, I haven't received it."
"Have you looked at your e-mail?"
"No."
"Please could you look at it. It will take you 10 minutes to read. Please ring me back when you have read it."

He rang me back within half an hour and I sponsored him.

You may find my approach to follow-ups rather uncomfortable to begin with. However, I've developed it with years of practice through talking to many, many people. It's effective because it means that you, as a sponsor, are more in control of the telephone call. I've taught this method to my team for years and it makes everyone who follows these principles instantly far more effective than they previously were. They sponsor more people, they get far less frustrated while communicating with potential prospects and it's extremely time efficient. It enables you to speak to more people in less time.

When you ring a prospect to do a follow-up you may get an answerphone. Always speak slowly and clearly taking particular care with your phone number. You may want to repeat it a second time.

Do not leave a long message. You don't have anything to hide, but if you leave a detailed message, for example, *"You responded to an advert ...."* nine times out of ten that person won't phone you back. They may have read your information, decided they don't want to join and you find it impossible to talk with them to cover objections. Your message should go like this;

"Hi Fred, it's John. Can you call me on xxxxx xxxxxxx. Thank you. Bye."

That's it. It works very well. Most people ring back because they don't know what it's about. If they don't, call the following day and leave a second message;

"Hi Fred, it's John, again. I rang you yesterday. Please can you get back to me on xxxxx xxxxxxx. Thank you."

You don't need to add to it. If you don't hear anything after three or four days, then make a final call. Keep it very polite and diplomatic and leave a message like this;

"Hi Fred, it's John. This is my third attempt to call you. I sent you an information pack in the post and you are obviously not interested. If you change your mind, please don't hesitate to call me. Once again, here's my phone number, xxxxx xxxxxxx. If I don't hear from you, I wish you all the success in what you do. Many thanks."

There are very good reasons for following-up this way. If you do many leads a week you can't continue to ring up every single one, night after night, until you speak to them. I was working with someone in my team recently and he said he had 40 follow-ups to do that night. I asked him if they were all fresh leads for today and he told me that 20 were from last week. This is not time effective.

When you leave a final message, one of two things can happen. Many people who receive this answerphone message call back and I've sponsored a good number of people this way, because I was given a chance to talk to them and cover objections. If the person does not call back they may be avoiding you or not at all interested.

Leaving a final message allows you to mentally move on. It's stressful to have 50 follow-ups to do in one night when many of them are trying to avoid you. Keep your message diplomatic. Some people do ring back and say *"Yes, I want to join"* or *"I have been away on holiday"*. The reason doesn't matter. When they call you, cover their objections, sponsor them or get referrals, try to sell them products, and then move on.

For this to be effective you must have call-minder and call-waiting. There is no point leaving a prospect a message asking them to call you back if you spend all evening on the telephone with other follow-ups.

Call-waiting is important because many people will phone you back within an hour of you leaving them an answerphone message. You are not being effective if your telephone is permanently engaged. You need a system where you can interrupt a phone call to answer their call immediately. It's really important because you may be on a phone call to one prospect and another is phoning you to tell you they are ready to join your business. I know of several high achievers in my network who joined with different legs because their first choice of up-line was permanently engaged on the telephone all evening. Many people are prospected by more than one person and these people called and joined with someone else.

You need to practice using call-waiting so that you don't get distracted while on the phone to prospects. Spend as short a time as possible with the second caller. Just find out their name, phone number and say you'll call them back after you have finished your other call.

Of course, if you are in a heavy conversation you have the option of ignoring the second call, so it is important you have call-minder to pick it up. However, many people will just leave you an answerphone message saying they are not interested and you may not get to cover objections.

Also, you still need a business answerphone for occasions when you are out or unable to answer your phone. I recommend you don't have the standard telephone provider answerphone script. It needs to be more personal, for example;

"Hi, it's John and Cathy. Unfortunately we aren't able to take your call at the moment. Please leave your name and number and we'll call you back as soon as we can. If it is urgent, my mobile number is xxxxx xxxxxxx." It works well and is very professional.

Follow-Up Flow Chart

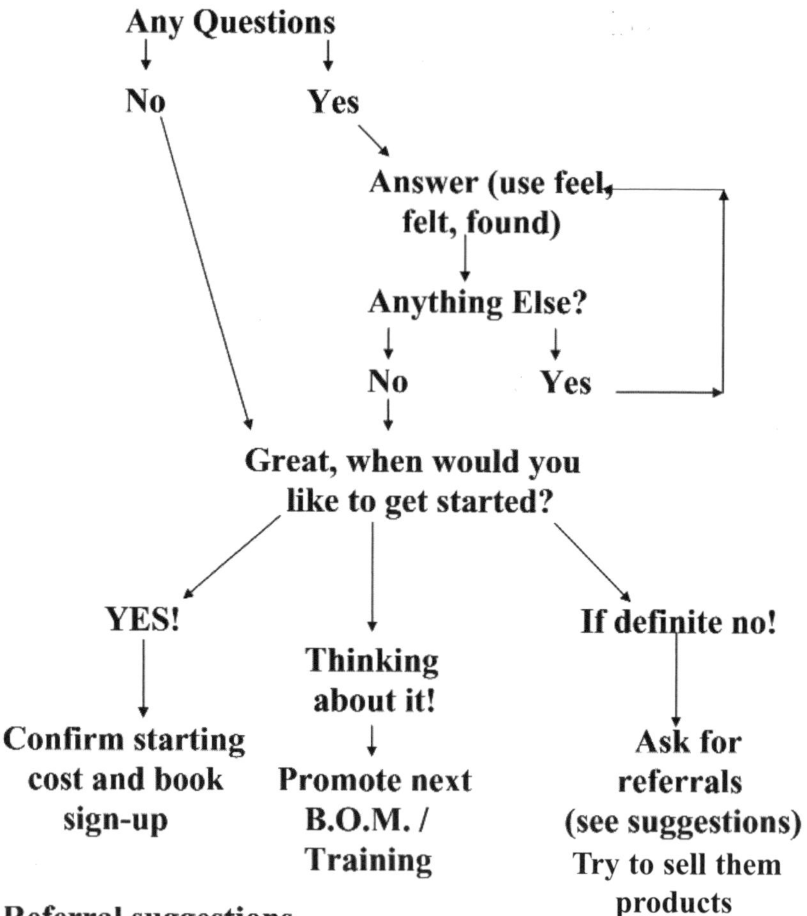

Referral suggestions

Do you know anyone who would like a second income?
Do you know anyone who has been in network marketing before?
Please pass the information on to someone who you think may be interested.
Try to sell them products

Feel, felt, found

I know how you feel, when I first started I felt…., but I found that…… .

Chapter 22

Making a Phone Call

Once your prospect has seen information on your business your follow-up phone call needs to be as effective as possible. It's easy to get frustrated with follow-ups if you can't speak to the person who responded to the advert, or you don't answer questions as effectively as you would like.

I'm going to give you practical and easy-to-use advice which I've been teaching for many years. It has proved to be extremely effective and has helped many people to excel at sponsoring. By putting this advice into action you will find follow-ups to be quicker, easier and more enjoyable.

Listening to your prospect on the phone is extremely important. I can talk for England but when I'm on the phone I'm quiet. I listen. I give out very little information over the phone because as far as I'm concerned it's all in the information pack.

When you are dealing with objections make sure you answer the question asked and don't go into too much detail.
For example, if a prospect asks you,
"Can you order on the internet?" your answer is *"Yes"*.
You don't need to spend ten minutes telling them how to do it.
"Yes" is the only answer you need to give.

If you tell people too much information it can be counter productive and you may actually talk people out of joining your opportunity.

One incident which happened about three years ago is particularly memorable. I was working with a team member using three-way calling. He was following-up a prospect and asked, *"Do you have any questions?"* to which the reply was *"Yes."*

The person I was coaching then answered the questions with far too much detail and was on the phone a very long time. The prospect he was talking to was not aware I was listening in so I tried to distract my down-line by coughing down the phone. It didn't work. He talked for so long that I actually made a cup of tea while he was on this call and he eventually talked the person out of joining!

When I coached him after the conversation I explained he had told his prospect too many details overwhelming him with information. There is a lot a prospect doesn't need to know before being sponsored. Remember to be brief,
"Can you order on the internet?" your answer is "Yes you can."
That's it. Don't give any more details on how to order.

If they ask, *"How do you order on the internet?"*
I'd say, *"No problem, all the information you need is in the registration kit. Get yourself some orders and I'll guide you from there. Let me get you started. Do you have a credit card?"* Keep it really simple.

Some prospects you contact won't be at all interested in your opportunity. Network Marketing isn't for everyone and you have to accept that and move on. With practice you will be able to identify these people very quickly and get off the phone. On a typical follow-up I'm off the telephone in thirty seconds, but if someone is interested I'd obviously take longer.

I'd also like to point out that I talk to the same types of people as you. Like you, I've had people put the phone down on me and others be rude, but I don't let them worry me or doubt my ability. If I feel anything for them it's sadness that they are not prepared to give the opportunity the respect it deserves, because I know it could change their lives for the better. When you get rejection on the telephone, prospects are not actually saying 'no' to you, they are saying 'no' to their future and 'no' to the opportunity.

When talking to prospects don't be afraid to use income stories. A small income can be powerful. Most people don't get a £200 a month pay rise in their job! The income does not need to be massive. A huge income is brilliant, but if a prospect has not joined or attended a training they will not be able to relate to a huge income.

At trainings I take notes on the stories of new distributors, why they have joined and what they are earning. Then, when I'm on the phone doing my follow-ups, I use these stories to sponsor people. I sponsor with their incomes, not mine. I don't tell prospects my monthly income or that I'm semi-retired. People can't relate to it. It's really important you understand this. If you are earning £200 a month from your opportunity it's a fantastic part-time income to many people. You have a powerful story.

Your follow-up phone call should be very simple and may start like this;

"Hi Mary, it's Peter. You responded to an advert in the newspaper and I e-mailed you / sent you an information pack in the post. Have you received it?"

Don't get into a lengthy conversation on which newspaper or advert it is. Keep it general. You want to move on to answering questions.

Chapter 23

Covering Objections and Follow-Up Situations

Prospects may tell you they are not interested in your opportunity because they have not read / watched your information pack properly, not fully understood it or are prejudging it. In this chapter I'll give you some scripts to use when you are covering the objections and excuses people come up with during follow-ups. These are sample responses which you can use as they are, or adapt to your opportunity.

Not read the information pack or watched the DVD?

The first thing you need to ask a prospect on a follow-up is, *"Have you read the information pack / watched the DVD?"*

If the prospect says no, inform him,
"It will take you 10 minutes to read / 20 minutes to watch. Could you please call me back once you have read it?"

By doing this you are controlling the phone call. You are effectively saying you don't need them, they need you. Then, if the prospect does not ring back, call him the next day to follow-up as usual. You are demonstrating the correct posture to your prospect. Never be rude or impolite.

My team and I have been using these techniques for many years. It works really well because it's simple. Many people do call you back.

Once you become comfortable with this approach, if your prospect has not looked at the information pack, you may also like to find out a little more information about your prospect.

If I sense they are a bit young, I actually say to people on the telephone, *"Are you working at the moment?"*

If their reply is, *"No"* I ask,
"May I ask why not? Why aren't you working?"

A prospect who says, *"No, I've not read it"* can also mean; *"No, it's network marketing, I'm not interested."*

Your answer should be, *"Do you know what we do?"*
"Yes!"
"Do you have any questions?"
"Great, when would you like to start?"

Keep it very simple. You may think this is very direct, but it gets the job done. One of two things will happen;

The person will say,
"Yes!" Ask them to read the information pack properly and then you sign them up.

Or *"No, it's not for me."*
Cover objections, ask for referrals and move on to the next follow-up.

I have not received the information pack!

First, check the address and postcode are correct. This is important because it could be wrong. If it's correct I say;

"No problem, it's on its way. You'll get it tomorrow. When you receive it tomorrow Peter, it will take you 10 minutes to read. Will you call me back please?"

Again, this is demonstrating the correct posture. If people want to join a business and become successful they want to join with people who are 'moving on'.

Posture is important. 'Moving on' doesn't mean you already have a big business. If you are doing what it takes, you are moving forward.

If the prospect hasn't received the pack you could also ask if they are on-line or have an e-mail address. If they do, offer to send an information pack in PDF format or ask them to look at your website.

It's not for me!

I have an excellent reply to this.

"Fantastic. It wasn't for me either. Peter, for my records I'd like to ask you what you don't like about it?" This opens the door for objections.

Don't be too eager to answer the objections straightaway. Follow the old adage 'one mouth and two ears'. It's really important you listen and don't answer immediately.
I would say;
"Peter, what don't you like about it?"
"Well, I don't like........."

Then I'd ask,
"Is there anything else you don't like about it? "
"Yes, I'm not sure about........"
"Anything else?"
"No, that's it."
"Ok,........."
Cover these objections. Keep it very simple and very positive. People understand you are positive and you want to help them move forward.

Continue the conversation,
"Peter, not a problem. You don't like ....(whatever it is)"

This next bit is the important bit. Take the emphasis away from the day to day activities, such as product sales and sponsoring, and ask him what income he would like to earn. It gets him thinking!

"But Peter, you responded to an advert to earn an extra income. How much would you like to earn?"

I regularly do this myself and sponsor people. A lot of people when they first view a network marketing opportunity only think about selling products.

"How much do you want to earn a month, Peter?"
"I want to earn £300."
"Well, Peter, I sponsored somebody / I know someone in the group who sponsored somebody last month who has done just that."

Use a recent story. Inform him;
"Peter, if people do as I teach them, they can earn £100 to £300 a month, part-time. Does that interest you?"
"When would you like to start?"

Sometimes I also ask a prospect,
"Are you sceptical?"
This can open the door to a conversation. You may want to tell them your story. Be truthful. Were you sceptical? Did you join straightaway? Did you have reservations?

Use 'feel, felt, found'.

"I know how you feel. When I first started I felt ...., but I found that............."

I have no money to start

First of all you need to ask,
"Is the money the only challenge you have? Is there anything else?"
You may find that 'no money' is actually an excuse and there are other objections.

You can inform them.
"Do you realise you can pay by credit card? You could get a bank overdraft or ask a family member?"

You may have heard stories where people have done everything they can to get the money to join your opportunity. Share these stories. If they say they really can't get the money, put the person to the test. You may choose to say to them,

"Is it really the only challenge? I want to help you. If you're serious and you really want to do something, I'd like to invite you to a training meeting. You can see whether the opportunity is for you and we can go from there."

Remember, before you get off the telephone ask for referrals. This is important.

I haven't got the time!

I have included below some of the ways you can cover this objection. Choose the one or ones which you feel comfortable with and which apply to your network.

- Direct Sales / Network Marketing / Your company name / What we do / This business is very flexible. It is designed to be built part-time alongside a job or other commitments.

- If you follow the system we have in place it is very time efficient.

- There are a lot of people in this industry who build their business part-time alongside their full-time job, people who also have children and in some cases, they don't even have a car. Do you think you could find 8-10 hours a week?

- Once you understand the concept of duplication you will appreciate that you don't have to do it full-time.

- Network Marketing / This business has not been designed to be worked full-time.

- You work it part-time until your income from Network Marketing overtakes your jobs wage or salary and then you can make choices about whether you want to do it full-time.

- I have learned that people who have full-time jobs often build much quicker than those who try to build a business full-time. Part-timers tend to work more focused in the hours that they have available to them to build their business.

- You only need 8-10 hours a week.

If the prospect has replied to an advert rather than been approached from a list you can say to them, "*You must have some spare time, or you wouldn't have applied for the advert.*"

You need to bear in mind that 'no time' can also be an excuse and they don't want to tell you "*No!*" At this point it would be good to ask them, "*Are you sceptical?*" as it will encourage them to ask other questions.

Cover with *feel, felt, found*!

"*I know how you feel. I felt the same way, but I found that......*"

Is it Pyramid Selling?

Definitely not! Pyramid selling is illegal!

Network Marketing is the modern way of organising a direct sales business where an income and rewards come from product sales and building a team. It is a very fair payment system. You get paid for the work you do, so if you do more work, you get paid more money. Unlike a job where it is highly unlikely that you will overtake the wage of your boss, in many cases in Direct Sales / Network Marketing people who joined later will earn more than the person who sponsored them in, because they do more work. You make your income by helping other people to achieve an income.

Speaking to a third party

Always speak to the person who asked for the information because it will save you loads of time.

"Hi, it's John, can I speak to Peter please."

Don't say, *"It's John Smith, can I speak to …."*
Use your first name because it's more personal and not so business orientated. Giving your full name makes the call very formal and leaves the way open for lots of questions such as,

"Why do you want to speak to him?"
"What's it about?"
"What's the name of your business?"

If you want to speak to Peter and his wife answers the phone, your conversation should go like this;

"Hello, is Peter there please?"
"Who's calling?"
"It's John, thank you."

It works. Once you have said 'thank you', nine times out of ten they don't ask any more questions.

If they are not in, you may be asked,
"He's not in, can I help you?"
"Yes. Can you ask him to give me a call please?"
"What's it regarding?"
"He knows. All the best. Bye" or
"It's to do with work he has applied for, thank you."

There is no point talking to Peter's wife because she'll probably not have read the information or be interested. You don't know at this point. Occasionally, the partner may be a little more insistent so you have to give them more information, but usually this works.

Your opportunity isn't a secret and you don't have anything to hide, but if you tell Peter's wife why you want to speak to him, when he gets home the conversation could go like this.

"John Smith rang about the information pack."
"I'm not interested."

Then, when you ring back the next day, the wife may stall you *"Peter is busy / not here / sunbathing in the garden."* Any excuse. Occasionally you'll be told *"No, he's not interested,"* but you won't get to speak to Peter.

You can ask to have a chat with him to find out why he's not interested, but usually you won't get the opportunity to cover objections or ask for referrals. You need to speak to the person who asked for the information.

You may find the responses I've shown you, and getting the correct posture on the telephone, will take you time to learn. Your telephone manner will improve with practice. If you think your telephone technique is not your strongest point you can compensate with increased activity until you improve. There are people in my team who have proved it. They may not have the best people skills but they speak to 100+ cold contact leads a week and they sponsor new distributors. Compensate with extra activity until you improve.

Lead / sponsor ratios really do improve with practice and continued self-development. They can improve so much you may sometimes sponsor one person a day. You need to focus on what you are doing. Focus is not a commodity of time. You don't need to work 18 hours a day.

Just make sure between 7 and 9 o'clock at night you do nothing but follow-ups and you do them effectively using the methods I'm teaching you in this book.

You must be speaking to enough cold contact, or warm market prospects each week to achieve your goals. Please don't delude yourself you can build your opportunity as big as you want to build it if you are not talking to enough people.

Network marketing is a fantastic opportunity for everyone. When I talk to prospects I'm offering them a chance to earn themselves a better lifestyle.

People who join my business are not joining for me, they are joining for themselves. If they don't want to join my team I talk to more people and sponsor those who want my help.

If you believe this and you have the correct posture you, too, will condition your mind for success. I believe sponsoring is easy. You just need to believe it. Enjoy using the telephone, enjoy talking and have fun.

Chapter 24

The 'Business Builder Sheet'

There are people in network marketing who earn phenomenal incomes. These people have all developed or followed a successful system to achieve their success.

For you to achieve a level of success in your own network marketing business you need to be using a successful system yourself. If you are not, it doesn't mean you will fail. You may get there, but it will take longer. Eventually, when you get frustrated and make the decision to build more quickly, you will use a simple, duplicatable system and speed up the growth of your business.

I had to develop my system. When I first started building my organisation I was helping people to build their teams by asking the same questions to every person I worked with. Once my team got bigger I realised I couldn't do everything for everyone, so I devised a sheet which asked the relevant questions and allowed my team to duplicate me, without needing me to be there. I call it a 'Business Builder Sheet'.

This sheet is simple to use and very effective if followed properly. It has a few basic questions on it which will help you, as the leader of your team, to work your business effectively, and it will help each person in your team to duplicate you. It saves a lot of time by identifying the people who are ready to build a business immediately. It speeds up the building process, creates momentum in a leg and helps to strongly secure the leg. Anyone using this 'Business Builder Sheet' regularly is actively building a business.

The sheet identifies what people truly want out of their business and then, when you have identified a potential builder, you both roll up your sleeves and get to work to achieve their goal. It also, very quickly, identifies the people who are not prepared to work.

As a leader you have your own goals to achieve. If your goal is to break two legs in twelve months, you know you have to identify two people who want to break in that time period. This sheet will enable you to identify these two people.

The format of the 'Business Builder Sheet' helps new distributors to create their goals and then plan the activity to reach them. It gives a new distributor confidence in you as a sponsor, as a coach and as a leader. It assures them you are there to help and that you genuinely want them to succeed. It's no good just telling people you want to help them. Actions speak louder than words and the positive inter-action gives new distributors a feeling of excitement and confidence within themselves.

By working through the sheet with each new distributor you will work out a plan of action, unique and suitable to each person and their time constraints, so they can begin to build a business.

Perhaps the biggest challenge you will encounter in network marketing is sponsoring people into your business who talk good and look good, but when you start to work with them you find they are not prepared to do what it takes to build a business. You get excited and then feel let down when they don't put their words into action. I've had many people claim they are going to build it big and then quit.

The 'Business Builder Sheet' sorts these people out very quickly. Once I have sat down with a new person to go through it, I know within a couple of weeks, if they haven't done what they said they would, that they are not yet ready to build a business. This isn't a problem. At least I know and I can move on. I can spend my time working with other people and when this person becomes ready I can work closely with them again.

Everyone has different goals. Using a 'Business Builder Sheet' and finding out the goals of your new distributors early on saves a massive amount of time with people who are not yet ready. Very few people admit to you they are not ready to build. Most will say they want to build a team but then they don't put in enough action to reach their goals. Some may be afraid of success or change, some may not know how to set their goals, and some may not know how to build a business and are too afraid to ask.

When you are going through the 'Business Builder Sheet' with your distributor you have to be honest. Your job, as a leader, is to help your team to reach their goals. Tell them what they need to do. You won't be helping them if you advise them incorrectly. I've spoken to people in the past who say they only have £50 a month to spend on advertising and they don't want to work their warm list. I say to them, "*Not a problem, but we need to move the length of time it will take you to achieve your medium-term goal from 6 months to 6 years.*" I'm very honest, and people respect honesty.

You may feel uncomfortable with some of the aspects of building a business I've described in this chapter. Honestly telling someone they won't reach their goals unless they do more business building activity can be uncomfortable. However, I have found that people often don't realise they are not doing what they need to do.

If you are not honest, people can get frustrated and leave the business because they think it isn't working for them! Honesty and integrity are very important.

Successfully going through the 'Business Builder Sheet' with each distributor will assist you in building your business much more quickly. You will be letting your distributors know you are right there with them, helping them every step of the way, until they can build without you.

It is very important to go through the 'Business Builder Sheet' sitting down one to one. If a distributor doesn't live locally to you I recommend you go through it after a training meeting. If they live reasonably close, you could meet them halfway or go to their home. Going through the 'Business Builder Sheet' on the telephone is far less effective because you can't see their sincerity for their business or their enthusiasm for their goals.

If someone won't go to trainings, teach them as well as you can over the telephone but don't go through the sheet. Once they get serious they will go to a training. Link up with them then.

If someone says to you they can't come to a training 'because of ...', or 'too far!' ask yourself, do they really want to build a team and earn a big income? I have people who travel over 300 miles to a training because they are serious about building their business.

When you go through the 'Business Builder Sheet' with a new person in depth, remember to take the sponsor or up-line of the new person with you. The first time, ask them to watch and take notes. Tell them, next time they will be doing it themselves.

The next time, let the sponsor go through the sheet and ask the questions with another one of their down-line. Coach the sponsor on what to say beforehand and tell them to ask the questions exactly and precisely as they are written on the

‘Business Builder Sheet’. Sit in with them, listen and take notes. This encourages complete duplication in your business. At the end, if they did anything completely wrong, ask the new person the questions correctly, yourself, so you have all the information you need. Then, when you and the up-line are alone, coach them further so they learn from their mistakes for the next time.

The third time, let them go through the ‘Business Builder Sheet’ with another new person on their own. Ask for an update of the information on goals and the date of the ‘Appointment to Build’. This way you are teaching them leadership, you are achieving duplication within your team and leveraging your time so you can teach another person to repeat the process.

The more distributors you have in your team who are capable of duplicating you with the ‘Business Building Sheet’, the stronger your business will be. A leg will be totally up and running once there are three levels of people building down the leg and using this sheet regularly and effectively.

Diagram 8

BUSINESS BUILDER SHEET

Step by step guide for new distributors.

QUESTIONS YOU SHOULD ASK WHEN YOU NEXT MEET

Setting Goals
What do you want out of this business?
(Establish short, medium and long-term goals)

Time Commitment
How much time are you prepared to commit to your business?

Product Sales / Movement
How much do you want to earn immediately from your business?
Tell them how much sales turnover / volume they will need to sell per month. (in £'s, points or number of products)

Sponsoring Training
Teach the methods of getting contact names of prospective distributors. Warm market list, business cards, 3 foot rule, press advertising, fliers, advertising pool, badges, car advert, shop window cards, mailing lists, etc.
EXPLAIN THE POWER OF THEIR WARM MARKET CONTACTS

Voice Mail
Check 3 times a day.

Building a Group
Advise how many people they need to contact per week.
Now book an 'Appointment to Build' to teach telephone script for list, follow-up for adverts, information packs, appointments / interviews, etc.
Sit down and work together or if not local do three-way calling.
Monitor progress regularly. (Initially every 48 hours).
Promote next training.

Carry a supply of sales aids to sell to new distributors before you leave.

Chapter 25

When is Someone Ready to go Through the 'Business Builder Sheet'?

Your new distributor needs to be involved in your network for a period of 1-2 weeks and must have sold some products to achieve a retail or income story. If they don't have a retail or income story you can't effectively go through the sheet with them.

Once your new distributor has a story, ask if they want to build a business. If they say "*No*" ask them, "*Why not?*" They may think they don't know anyone or have other concerns. Ask if they have a desire to earn an extra income? Would they like to build a team? Let them know you can help them.

If the person is adamant that they just want to earn a small income from selling products, keep an eye on them. Send them newsletters or CD's and try to get them onto your voicemail system. Always promote trainings. Keep in touch and support them until they are ready to build a business. Everyone is ready at different stages.

I have one couple in my team who were very reluctant to attend a training or to team build. I kept an eye on them until they were ready to move forward. They finally decided to attend their first training and they haven't missed one since. They went on to build a big business. Keep people on the back burner until they are ready.

Ask your new distributor if they would like to build a business. Don't tell them, "*....book an appointment to go through the Business Builder Sheet.*" The unfamiliar terminology may confuse them. It's an appointment to teach them how to build their business.

If they say they want to build a business, promote the next training to them. Make an appointment to sit down together afterwards to go through the 'Business Builder Sheet' or book an appointment at your home or their home if you are local to each other.

Chapter 26

Going Through the 'Business Builder Sheet'

The 'Business Builder Sheet' is very important. It's how you work with your team effectively and how you teach your team to duplicate you.

Go through the questions one at a time, exactly as they are written on the 'Business Builder Sheet'. Be precise and make sure you have the answer to each question before you move on to the next one.

First, find out the new distributor's short-term, medium-term and long-term goals. If you can earn a reasonable income on a part-time basis, purely from selling products in your opportunity, try to tie-in the short-term goal with the retail income. Tie-in the medium-term goal with the volume of activity they are prepared to do to build their business.

Then find out their time commitment. Make sure they are prepared to devote enough time to their business to reach the goals they said they wanted to achieve.

There have been occasions when I haven't completed the sheet with someone because they said they wouldn't be prepared to put in enough time to build their business. If this happens, say to them,

"That's OK, but you said you wanted these short-term, medium-term and long-term goals. I'm here to help you to do this, but this is what you need to do to achieve them."

And go no further with the sheet. Be very polite. They are not ready to build a business yet, and knowing it saves you time.

After establishing the distributor's goals and time commitment, advise them what volume of personal sales they need to do in a month to reach their short-term goals. This is because you are tying in the short-term goal with product sales, if it is possible.

Next you need to briefly go through methods of getting contact leads for sponsoring people. Advise them there are two ways of building; the warm market, cold contact adverts or they may wish to do a combination of both. Try to get them to work their list. Stress that it's the quickest and cheapest way to build. Tell them stories to demonstrate the power of working their list. I always give my story, and recent stories of people in my team.

If you use a voicemail system tell them about its benefits and, if you can, get them to sign the paperwork to join immediately. Advise them what to put in the personalised greeting and tell them to speak clearly and precisely.

Finally, the last thing you do is book an 'Appointment to Build'. This is where you roll up your sleeves and really get to work. It's an appointment to sit down together or do three-way calling if your new distributor doesn't live locally to you.

This 'Appointment to Build' is when you teach your new distributor how to build their business. Booking this appointment is the most important part of the 'Business Builder Sheet'.

If you don't book the 'Appointment to Build' all the information you have covered in the rest of the sheet is a waste of your time. You won't be progressing to the next level of building their business with them. Very few people will build a business on their own. You need to teach them how to build their business effectively and support them until they are up and running and confident they can do it.

Start by saying to them,

"Now we are going to start building your business. How would you like to build your business to achieve your goals? The list is the fastest and cheapest way to build. Are you happy to work your list?"

Find out their answer, then choose a day for the 'Appointment to Build'. For example,

"OK, today is Saturday. We will start making calls on Thursday."

The 'Appointment to Build' must be made within a week of going through the 'Business Builder Sheet' so they don't go cold.

At this point, if they are happy to work their warm list and you both have the time, help them to start drafting their list. Refer to chapter 12, 'Drafting Your Warm Market Contact List'.

Ask your down-line to post or e-mail their list to you before the 'Appointment to Build' and make sure the initial phone calls are done effectively so people attend.

On Thursday, the day of the 'Appointment to Build', make phone calls. I've covered 'Helping Your Down-line To Work

Their Contact List' in Chapter 17, so I won't go into detail here. However, remember that you must be involved in the planning of any house meeting.

If your down-line is unwilling to work their list at this point you must still book an 'Appointment to Build.' Use it to teach follow-ups or appointments using cold market contacts.

Whether or not a person chooses to work their contact list is up to them. If you are working with a down-line who doesn't want to work their list, tell them what they need to do to reach their medium-term goal, bearing in mind you tie-in the medium-term goal with the activity they put into building their business. Use your experience to advise them what activity they need to do and how many contacts or leads they need to speak to per week. Say to them,

"That's OK, we'll start building your business using advertising. You need to speak to XXX people a week to achieve your goals."

You need to get them started with lead generating activity quickly. Give them a selection of sales aids with the aim of generating an immediate response from prospects, so you can follow-up or book appointments on Thursday.

You may want to give them fliers, cards or other sales and recruiting aids to get them started. Advise them how to get their own personalised web site with their picture and story on it. If they want to place their own local adverts, advise them what wording to use. Let them know how they can become part of an advertising pool.

You may be in the position to say to them,

"I'm running a couple of adverts at the moment. They cost me £100 a month. If you give me £50 I'll give you half the leads which come in."

Refer to Chapter 18 on 'Cold Market Advertising' for other ideas to generate cold market leads.

Make sure you kit your distributor up with everything they need. Sell or give them information packs, CD's, DVD's or an opportunity presenter. Depending on which method you use, arrange for them to attend an appointment or interview with you to learn how to do a presentation or, if you teach posting information packs, advise them they must be sent first class and followed-up one to two days later. Give them a sample covering letter and let them know it's important to keep it very short and simple so the prospect looks at the written information, CD or DVD to see the full picture.

Monitor them every 48 hours until the day of the 'Appointment to Build', to make sure they are doing what they said they would do. This will enable you to check they are successfully generating cold contact leads, so you can teach them to follow-up or make appointments on the Thursday.

48 hours before the 'Appointment to Build' send them a follow-up flow chart, (see 'diagram 7') or a script. The follow-up flow chart is easy to follow and reminds them what to do. Connect together using 'three-way calling' to make phone calls.

After the 'Appointment to Build' continue to monitor their progress for the next couple of weeks until they are confidently building on their own and teaching their down-line to duplicate you. Support them from here to check they stay on target. You need to remember that by helping them to achieve their goals, you will achieve yours.

Chapter 27

Working in Depth

I still choose to spend some of my time building my network marketing business. However, when I sponsor new distributors, I'm now in the position where I don't need to take them front-line to me. Everyone I sponsor is placed strategically in my team with people who are working hard and following my system. I have a few reasons for this. Placing people in depth increases the strength and security of a leg, I have leaders in place who can work with the people I sponsor and also, I want to help the people in my team to achieve their own success.

What I do now is different to what I did when I first started my network marketing business. Back then I sold a lot of products, I earned a good income from sales and I worked very hard to build a team. Now, I own my life and I do a lot less with the business. When I work in my business I spend less time selling products and more time coaching my down-line. However, I still practice every aspect of network marketing, including selling a small amount of product each month, because I believe leading from the front is the best way forward.

I believe in empowerment, I believe in duplication, I believe in teaching and I believe in making people independent very quickly. If I did everything for my distributors I wouldn't have the business I have today. You won't reach a high level in network marketing if you build a business **'for'** the people in your team, rather than **'with'** them. To be successful you have to work closely 'with' the keen people in your team and teach them to duplicate you. You have to help them to become successful by teaching them to become independent. I believe leaders are not born, they are developed!

Working in depth creates security and momentum. You build friendships because you are working down at the bottom of a leg as though you had personally sponsored that person. If you have a down-line whose sponsor has quit, I also believe you have a moral obligation to help them. They joined your organisation and will be looking to you.

Network Marketing is only a numbers game until you find someone to work with. Once you sponsor someone, from this point onwards you have to work with them and help them to achieve their goals. You can't have the philosophy 'I've sponsored a big fish, so I'll let them get on with it on their own'.

This happened to me. My sponsor quit a few weeks after I started and I was left to get on with it on my own. I learned the hard way. I made many mistakes and eventually I developed a system to build my network.

We are not recruitment consultants. You can't sponsor people into your business and then leave them to build a business on their own. It makes sense for you to roll your sleeves up and work with them because two people working in the same business will make it grow more quickly. When you work with your down-line have the attitude,
"Great, I'm going to 'work with' and help this person, but I'm still going to sponsor other people as well."

Offer your team your full support, help and commitment. Of course, if someone does not want your help there isn't much you can do.

You need to be straight, honest and polite with people you work with. Say to them,

"This is your goal. I can help you but this is what you have to do, a, b and c."

When you look for people to 'work with', look for those who are plugging into your system, who are selling products, attending trainings and willing to work with you to build a team.

The work you do with these people will determine how successful they will be and in turn, how successful you will be. You can't just recruit people and abandon them. If you sponsor a person you roll your sleeves up and 'work with' them, teaching them how to build a business. When everyone works together you create momentum in your business and everyone involved earns a bigger income. It's important you work with people effectively. If you don't it takes a long time to teach your team, and growth in your business will be slower.

When you sponsor people don't give them all the information they need to build their entire business in one go, because you will drown them with information. You teach a person to build a business by drip feeding them, step by step. I have learned that confused distributors don't build a business.

I want to give you an example of information overload. A while ago I had a couple in my team who thought it was a great idea for their new distributors to have all the information they would need to build their network marketing business, as soon as they joined their team. Every time they sponsored someone they gave them a big manual with the sign up pack and they blew a lot of people out of their business, before they got started, with information overload.

You have to keep it simple. Drip feeding information, bit by bit, is always better. You don't throw a loaf of bread to a pigeon. You break it into small manageable chunks.

I teach my team to sponsor new distributors with the starter pack from the company and just one sheet of paper, which I call the 'Start Right Sheet'. I have included a sample copy in 'diagram 9'. I recommend you give something similar to your new distributors to get them started quickly and smoothly.

If you want to lose a distributor, don't talk to them.

Regular communication with your team members is vital. When you speak to them always be positive. Never, never be negative. Being negative will make people doubt whether they can become successful or achieve financial security with your network marketing company, or with you as their up-line.

Using the correct vocabulary to people is also important. For example, when you talk to your team always refer to 'trainings' rather than 'meetings'. Many people, especially those who have never attended a training before, are scared by the thought of attending a meeting, or they may consider it unimportant to attend because they don't understand why they are going. By saying to people,

"There is a training on Saturday which will help you to build your business",

you are using the correct vocabulary. The training will become important to them.

Diagram 9

Start Right Sheet

Distributor Name ______________________

Distributor Number ______________________

Sponsors Name ______________________

Telephone Number ______________________

Up-line Sponsors Name ______________________

Telephone Number ______________________

Monthly Income £

Week 1 activity planner retail sales / sponsoring activity.

Monday	Tuesday	Wednesday	Thursday	Friday	Saturday	Sunday

Next training Date ______________

Venue ______________

Time ______________

Current Company / Group Promotions ______________________

Other important notes ______________________

You may also wish to include on the 'Start Right Sheet' details like your group name as a header, group web / e-mail address, a company service centre contact number, first book / CD you recommend they listen to or a few pointers to follow when they are selling products or doing sponsoring activity.

Welcome to the Team

Chapter 28

Become a Leader

When you 'work with' your team, always look at and 'work with' people at the bottom of each leg in your business. You need to teach your team to duplicate you effectively, so you can develop your business properly. Once you do this, you can walk away from the legs which are built and they will continue to grow without you. The reverse is also true. You may be great at selling products or excellent at recruiting new people into your team, but if you don't 'work with' effectively, you won't leverage your time and your business will stop growing.

Ultimately, it's up to you to make your business succeed. I hear people say, "*I haven't got the right up-line to work with!*" or "*I need a good person in my group to build a business!*"

Do you? Yes? No?

My attitude is, become the person building a big business and you will become a magnet. Like attracts like. You attract people who want to be like you, those who are motivated and who are keen to build a business.

If you feel no-one in your team is doing enough for you to reach your goals don't give up. Wait for pay day. Use the information you read in this book to help you to become a good leader. Don't expect your team to get moving quickly and then follow them.

Become the person they can duplicate and some of the people in your team will develop and grow. As a sponsor you need to lead from the front. You are there to help your down-lines to develop an income. Carry on sponsoring people yourself and very quickly you will sponsor people who want to run with you at your speed.

Leaders don't make excuses. You have to make it happen. I believe in the saying,

If it's going to be, it's up to me.

You must take full responsibility for your business. By doing this, if some people drop out of your team you won't lose your income or your lifestyle.

To grow your business you need to keep sponsoring new distributors and work effectively with the new people in your team. If you don't, you may sponsor many people but most will leave your business as quickly as you sponsor them in.

Working in depth anchors legs and keeps a network marketing business driving forward. Teach everyone in your team to give you contact details of any new distributors they sponsor. It's important to give all new distributors a 'Welcome Call' when they join your team. Introduce yourself, tell them your story and leave them your contact details.

A 'Welcome Call' says more than just *"Hello, welcome to the team."* It lets your new distributor know there is a whole team helping them to get started and ready to work with them to build their business. The call starts to build trust and friendship which you need to 'work with' your down-line and build a team. It creates effective leadership which is interlinked with fast growth and anchoring your business strongly and securely.

When you are talking to a new distributor on the 'Welcome Call' briefly assess what the person is expecting to achieve out of their business. You may want to keep an eye on them as prospective 'keen' people to 'work with' in the near future.

Once you have someone in your down-line who is very competent, perhaps reaching the first important level in your marketing plan, teach this down-line how to make a 'Welcome Call' to new people sponsored into their group. This, once again, is duplicating you and leveraging your time.

You need to remember this rule.

**The less you work with your distributors,
the less they will work with their distributors.**

'Working with' doesn't mean you do everything for the people in your team. You should not 'mother hen'. (Do it all for everyone because you want everything done correctly). Leaders are very good at encouraging people. 'Work with' your team and communicate with them regularly. You need to develop people to become good leaders.

Chapter 29

Developing a Business

The more people you have duplicating you in your team, the quicker your business will grow. Duplication creates independence and leadership. If you choose not to follow these principles it will slow the growth of your team.

When I talk about securing or anchoring a leg to give your business a solid foundation you need to remember that a leg is not just one person. One person is a distributor. A leg is three to five 'keen' distributors deep. Once you start to build a leg, you are creating momentum within your business and you need to start working in depth.

Choose the strongest person to 'work with'. Once you have chosen this person, work with them as though they are front-line to you. However, when you work with this person, make sure you also include their sponsor. Don't make the mistake of by-passing the sponsor of the person you are working with, unless the sponsor isn't doing anything in the business.

When you are 'working with' somebody in your team, I recommend you have a diagram of their team in front of you as a reference. Circles are easy to read.

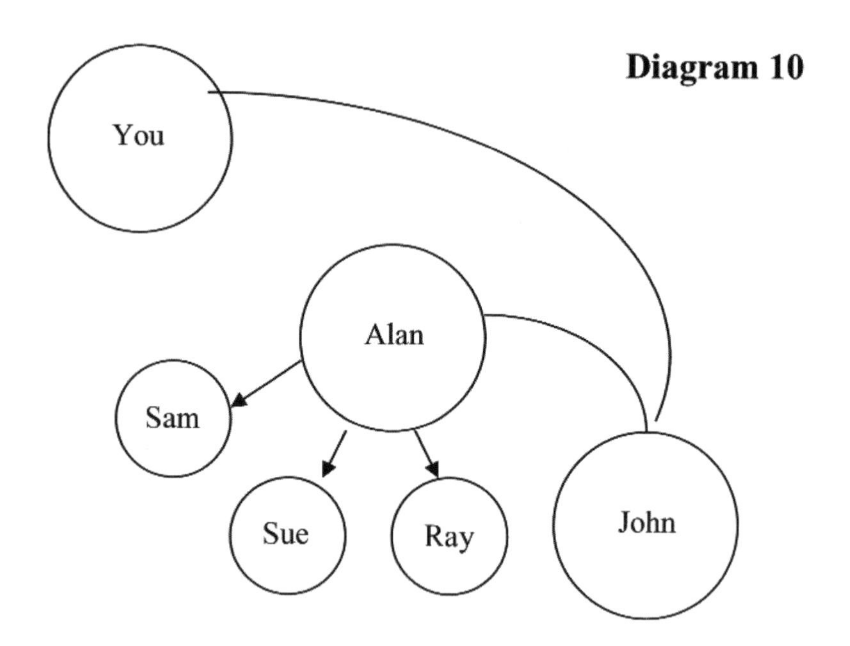

Here is an example. You sponsor Alan, and Alan sponsors John. You work with John and include Alan in everything you teach John, so Alan learns what you are doing and can duplicate you on his second, third, and fourth legs.

You work in Alan's strongest leg 'with' Alan which, in this example, is John. Build one leg **'with'** Alan, teaching him how to duplicate you, and then **'help'** him to build his width.

Teach Alan how to start John off correctly. Alan teaches John how to sell products and to get a retail story. 7-14 days after John starts, once he has a retail story, you and Alan sit down with John and go through the 'Business Builder Sheet'. You are teaching Alan how to 'work with' John.

When John sponsors his first person (Mary in the following example), Alan teaches John to go through the 'Start Right Sheet' with Mary. Be involved, either in the same room with them or on a three-way telephone call.

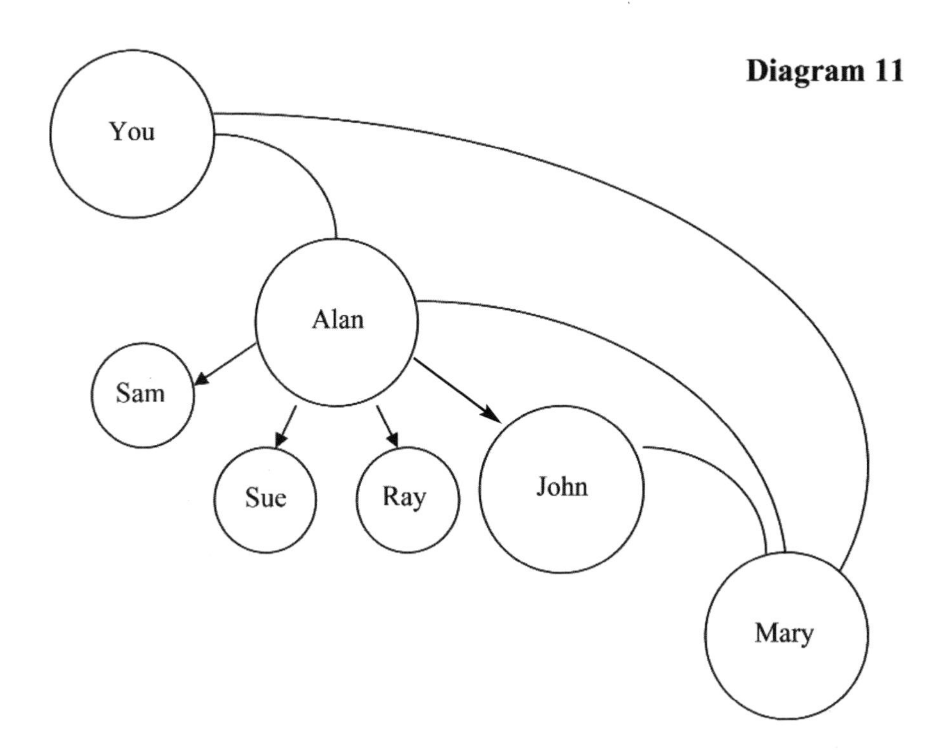

Check Alan is teaching John to duplicate you and they are both 'working with' Mary correctly.

If you build the first leg **'for'** someone rather than **'with'** them, you will need to build their second and third legs for them, because they won't know what to do. If you work with John, but you don't teach Alan how to work with John, then you are not getting duplication. Alan doesn't know what to do. You have all got to work together! As long as you are teaching the distributor you are 'working with' to teach the distributor they are 'working with' and to keep repeating the process your team is duplicating you.

Here is an example of how you 'work with' Alan to help John to build his business.

"Alan, I'm going to start John off on the phone, working his list. Can you please take notes because the next time you will be doing it."

You are not putting the sponsor, Alan, under pressure but you are creating leadership. He is aware that next time he sponsors someone he will be the person helping them to work their list on the phone, with your help of course. The first time you show them what to do, tell them to take notes and the next time they do it with your guidance.

If Alan stops working and loses focus, you still need to try and include Alan when you are working with John. You can say to Alan,
"Come and help me work with John, it's your business so let's do it together."

It may motivate Alan but if he doesn't want to continue working with John, just give Alan an up-date. Using this method, on many occasions I've turned disillusioned, unfocused distributors into keen and focused distributors who have gone on to build a business.

Keep working down a leg until you are duplicated in it by other people. You need to ask yourself,
"Am I being duplicated, or am I doing it all for them?"

Are you teaching your leaders to duplicate you, or are you sponsoring people for them and mother-henning? You have to make sure you are being duplicated.

Sponsoring new people and placing them with down-line is important when you are 'working with' someone, but you need to make sure that they have proved themselves capable of looking after a new person by sponsoring one or more people themselves first. You need to be confident that the new person will be looked after correctly, allowing you to leverage your time and work with other people.

It may not necessarily be a front-line person, sponsored by you, who progresses to building a big business. I have many large legs in width and I only sponsored the front-line leaders in one of these legs myself. The front-line leaders of the other legs joined because I work in depth. People I worked with led me to other people to work with. Then, the leaders rolled-up to my front-line after their sponsors quit. Working in depth is often how you find and develop your leaders.

Chapter 30

Focus on Your Team

You should always have more than one keen distributor in your business to 'work with' in depth. Having multiple legs to choose from and more than one keen distributor to 'work with' stops you 'mother-henning' and strangling the growth of people you are working with. Try to have 5 'open businesses', separate front-line distributors or groups outside of any broken legs, so you have a choice of who you 'work with'.

This ensures you don't put pressure on any one person to work at your speed. You can't push people to work more quickly than they want to, in order for you to achieve your goals in the time-frame you require. You need to find people who want to work as quickly as you do. You need choice!

I had the same challenge in my early days of building. I learned to steer the focus away from my business and how the success of my down-line would help me to achieve my goals. Now, when I work with someone I work in their business and focus on their goals.

Focus on helping your down-line to make money for themselves and to achieve their goals, not on how much you will make. Yes, I know it's difficult. You start your network marketing business and you want to make a lot of money!

It's hard to change your thinking and steer focus away from yourself at first, but you need to help someone to get what they want forgetting about yourself. By doing this and genuinely helping other people to become successful it will come back to you ten-fold. By helping distributors in your team to succeed you will automatically succeed yourself.

How do you do this? If your goal is to achieve the first step in your company's marketing plan, try not to focus on it, because even though you are working with your down-line, you are effectively focusing on your own goals.

Look ahead to the future. Help the distributor you are working with, to focus on helping two people in their width or front-line to build a foundation to break two legs, or to achieve the first step in the marketing plan.

In other words, (see diagram 12) you should not focus on,

(i) your front-line distributors achieving the first step on your company's marketing plan, but on

(ii) helping two of their down-line

(iii) to help two people in their front-line to achieve the first major step in the marketing plan.

Once they get close to achieving this level, teach them to help another two distributors so that they keep re-setting their goals slightly higher, each time.

Always focus two steps ahead. This will help you to achieve the security of a good royalty income. If you have two strong legs duplicating you in your business, with a good structure, you can leave town. Your business will continue to grow without you. Your team will be earning money and confident they can achieve their goals. In time you will achieve your goals more quickly.

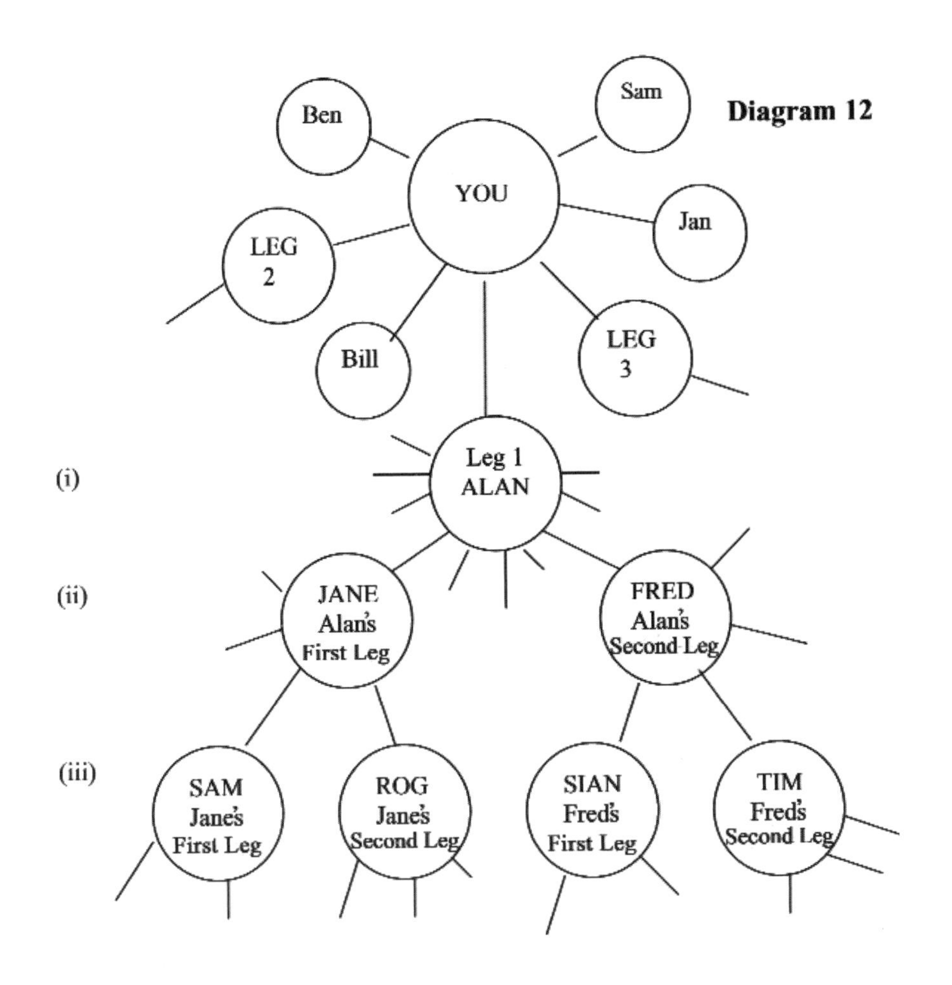

Going through the 'Business Building Sheet' with your team members will identify those who want to build their business **today**. If you have the choice of several 'keen' people to work with you won't put any one person you are working with under pressure to build at your speed. If the person you are working with stops doing what they need to do to achieve their goals, you can move on to the next 'keen' person.

Always concentrate on the keenest person first. If you have two or three in width who are equally very keen, initially concentrate on the one who has someone keen in depth. This is the leg you should be working with.

It is essential to develop and anchor one leg at a time. A leg needs to be properly secured by having three levels of builders who are duplicating you and doing what it takes. The first builder could be front-line to you, but then the next builder in that leg could be 3, 4 or even 10 levels in depth. Once you have built your team this way and it's growing without you, you will leverage your time and be free to build other legs.

You do this by spending 80% of your time working with one person for a maximum of one to two months. After this time they should be competent enough at duplicating you and teaching their down-line, for you to move on to a new person or a different leg. Even though you have moved on, you still continue to support them if they need your help.

If you have people in your team who are not, right now, doing what it takes to build their business at a fast pace, keep them on the back-burner because everyone develops at different stages. Distributors who are not creating the necessary activity to achieve their goals can still lead you to other people to work with, or in the future they could develop and do what is required to build a big business. Work lists, teach, keep in communication, help and support these distributors but only spend 20% of your time with them.

Chapter 31

Who Do You Work With?

You need to make sure the person you choose to work with is plugging into your trainings. If somebody is committed but they don't attend trainings, they are not ready and you can't work with them effectively. They must come to trainings or it will be very difficult for them to learn how to build their business. A carpenter's apprentice has to go to work every day or he won't learn his trade. It's the same with network marketing. You need to view your business as a trade or a career.

The person you are 'working with' doesn't necessarily need to live locally to you. You can still work together very effectively using three-way calling. With the technology available today it's not time efficient to travel all over the country to teach your team.

The person you choose to work with is often a new distributor, but may be someone who has been in your team for a number of years. I've had people come to me four or more years after starting and say they are now ready to build a business seriously.

Whether new or established, the person you are working with needs to be communicating with you on a regular basis and if you have a voicemail system in place they should be using it effectively and checking it regularly.

During a new distributor's first couple of weeks you should speak to them on the telephone on a regular basis, at least every two days. You will get a rapport going between you and this will allow you to address any challenges quickly.

When distributors first join your voicemail system they need to get used to using it. Leave them a voicemail message on the day they join your system with advice on how they can respond to you.

Then, leave a message every day and ask them to respond to you so that they get used to using the system. This way they will see the benefit of having a voicemail and want to keep it.

The way a distributor uses the voicemail system can be a measure of how serious they are about their business. There have been occasions when I've left a message for a team member and received the reply three days later. I question how serious this person is about their business. How many cold contact leads have they lost? Don't copy over advertising leads to a down-line if you are not sure they will follow them up.

Teach your team to put any advice you give them into action immediately. I work with distributors who put information they hear on voicemail or at a training into action immediately.

The person you are working with also needs to be selling an acceptable number of products per month. The actual volume of product sales is up to them but they should be earning an income, even if it's only a small one, from personal sales. If they are not selling products they won't be earning an income and, ultimately, they are not going to be in the business very long.

They also need to be sponsoring themselves. They need to be working their list and / or doing their own lead generating activity, and proving to you they are the correct person for you to work with.

If you have lead overload, in other words, more cold market contacts than you can cope with, you may consider giving the person you are 'working with' some of your leads to leverage your time.

You should also place some of the people you personally sponsor, into their business. It's important you choose the people you 'work with' carefully as you need to know they are capable of looking after the new people you place with them effectively, with your help.

However, 'working with' does not mean you stack people you sponsor one under another. If you build a leg without the security of builders in depth your business could yo-yo or even crumble. Place new distributors strategically with people who are already building themselves to strengthen their business. It also gives the new person an extra up-line to help and support them while building their business.

It is really important to work with 'serious' distributors. Building a strong leg with someone can take time, even 1 or 2 years, but in the end you will have a very solid and secure business. You need to achieve a balance between your needs right now and the speed at which you want to build a secure future for yourself.

Don't waste time with talkers. You can find out who these people are by going through the 'Business Builder Sheet', see 'Diagram 8'. If you follow the sheet correctly, it will help you build a leg naturally.

I want to share a story with you. A couple of years ago I was helping someone in my team to plan a house meeting. Two days before the meeting he had a major personal challenge and he cancelled it. I completely understood...... until I rang him up and found he was at work.

I knew at this point, this distributor was not ready to build a serious business. If his personal challenge meant he couldn't carry on with his business, how was he able to go to work?

He was taking his daytime job more seriously than his part-time business. This is not the way to succeed. A network marketing business is a part-time business but it has to be treated with a full-time attitude. Someone who is serious about their business and the goals they want to achieve, must treat their network marketing business as a high priority. I believe that if there is a crisis and someone can't build their business, they shouldn't go to work either.

A job gives you an immediate income, but your network marketing business is able to give you a better lifestyle in the future. How important is this to you?

Your team need to understand that you have to 'work with' people who are ready to work with you today. If you don't have anyone to 'work with' in your team, sponsor people yourself until you do.

It is important to keep sponsoring people yourself while you are 'working with' people in your team for two reasons. Firstly, if you are working down a leg with one of your distributors, that leg will grow a lot quicker with two of you sponsoring new people into the leg. Secondly, not everyone in your team will do what they said they would to achieve their own goals and you need to make sure you are able to keep moving on to achieve yours.

It is important that people in your team see you, and also other members of your team, growing and progressing up the marketing plan because it gives them belief they can be successful, too. If they don't see you moving on, it's not motivating for them.

If you are really committed, the fastest you can put the foundation for a new leg in place is three to four weeks. It's still done part-time but it needs to be done properly, making no excuses and using focused tunnel vision.

Look to the future. Don't only focus on what is happening in your business today. Focus on tomorrow and the next 12 - 18 months. Visualise how you want your business to develop. You have to see it. I recommend you draw circles of how you want your team to be, on paper, and build your team to that structure.

Enjoy working with your team. If you feel there are things you haven't done correctly in the past, don't worry. You can't do anything so wrong it can't be rectified later on. It's far better to do something and get it wrong than never to do it at all. Learn by your mistakes so next time you do it right. Network Marketing is very forgiving.

It doesn't matter how wrong you do it, you can start again and do it more effectively next time. People who are successful in network marketing will have had plenty of practice before they became good at what they do.

Chapter 32

You Can Make It Happen

You can either make excuses or you can make money, but you can't make both.

You need to know your reason for building a network marketing business. It may be cars, houses, leaving your job, investments, or you may want it all. Once you have built your network and are earning a royalty income, you can choose what you want to do with your life. It can all be yours.

But first you have to build your business. You must know what your goals are for the next 12 to 24 months. They don't have to be big goals. Small goals are important too, but they must be important to you. Are you confident you can now achieve them? You need a written plan of action otherwise you will be continuously chasing your tail.

Your plan needs to be broken down into the activity you need to do on a daily basis to enable you to reach your goals. Then, you need to do the activity you have written down on your plan of action, every day, persistently and consistently, until the goal is achieved. Put into action the successful activities I have shared with you in this book.

The key to achieving your goals is simply to get out there and do what it takes to achieve them. Set yourself a challenge today. Write a weekly planner and tracker with massive activity, then work it every day for three months. You will see your business completely turn around and your income will grow massively.

Some people give up on their goals! Always wait for pay day. Never, ever give up.

I've had people in my organisation who quit just after sponsoring distributors who went on to build a big business. The people who quit did not receive the benefit of sponsoring a good person.

I was recently working with someone on their contact list and I saw the name of a person who had been in my business, but quit, not long after I started networking. If he had remained in my business today, he would have had one of the largest legs in my organisation because his down-line went on to build a big team and become very successful. He left before pay day. The moral of the story is never, ever quit.

You need to be persistent and consistent while striving towards your goals. You can't do activity for just one week or one month at a time and keep stopping. Many people create the necessary activity to reach their goals for a short period of time and then they stop. Then they carry on again for a short period of time. Then they stop again. Every time you take a break from activity you lose all the momentum in your business. Consistent activity on a regular basis is imperative to reach your goals.

The effort you put into your business and the work you do now will achieve tangible results in about three months. You have to continue with constant and regular, daily activity, until you have reached your goal.

There is no luck in this industry. You create your own luck. You actually have to go out, roll your sleeves up, work your business and then you will earn the money.

Doing massive activity will make you lucky!

Focus on daily activity. If you have a regular job, your boss has a plan for you to follow. You have to be disciplined and focused on daily activities for your employer, for 40+ hours a week.

The only difference with running your own business is you need to be disciplined for yourself and be your own boss. In your available time, evenings and weekends, choose to do it for yourself. Be disciplined and work as hard for your future as you have to for your employer.

You need to help those who 'deserve' your time, not those who say they 'need' it. If you work with people who 'need' the business, or 'need' the money, but don't 'deserve' your help because they are not doing what it takes, you can get side tracked and lose focus on your goals. Using the 'Business Builder Sheet' will identify these people quickly.

You need to sponsor people and teach them how to duplicate you, to sponsor people themselves and become the leader of a team of distributors. It really is quite simple. A big group equals a big income. This is the vision I have, along with many other people who have achieved phenomenal incomes with network marketing.

Treat your business as a business, not as a hobby and give it the respect it deserves because it can make you very wealthy. If you would like next year to be more successful than this year you have to put more energy into your actions. A network marketing business is energy driven so get your head down and start charging.

If you don't have the motivation to do something, do what you don't have the motivation to do and the motivation will come.

You may think you need to be motivated to make phone calls, to work your contact list, or to go to a training. It's the other way round. If you make the phone calls, work your list and go to the training then the motivation comes. Focusing on your goals will help to give you the motivation you need to do your activity.

Avoid procrastination and become a person who does things 'right now'. Never wait for tomorrow if you can do it today. Discipline is vitally important in building your business. Some people spend hours procrastinating on computers or analysing things prior to starting their activity, and in some cases this leads to them never starting. Don't analyse. Just get out there and do it. If you become a 'doer', things start falling into place. Do what needs to be done immediately and you can learn to do it more effectively each time you do it.

Network Marketing is a proven industry and it has been making people money for many years. Your personal achievement is up to you. You need to make your dreams come true. It's not your sponsor's or your up-line's responsibility. They are only there to help and guide you. Ultimately, the responsibility for your success is with you!

Believe in your ability to build a network marketing business and don't feel negative or get bogged down with details. Building a network marketing business is not a walk in the park. It's a very serious income generating business and you have to take it seriously.

You need to understand the concept of duplication and put the training you receive into action.

Remember, your future is in your hands. If you don't do the necessary activity from today, right now, you will be in the same position next year as you are in today.

Know your reason for joining network marketing and drive towards your goals. If you really desire a bigger income and a more financially secure future, you can make it happen.

I wish you all the success in your network marketing business.

Copies of this book can be
ordered directly from the author
using the link on the website or
by emailing the address below.

Bulk discounts are
available to group leaders.

Free downloads of the worksheets
in this book can be found on the website,

www.the-formula-for-success.com

sales@the-formula-for-success.com

Filament
Publishing